ROUND-U

CH00925880

CONTENTS

Introduction

Round-up Grammar Practice 3 combines games and fun with serious, systematic grammar practice. It is ideal for students of English at the early stages of language learning.

Students see grammar points clearly presented in colourful boxes and tables. They practise grammar through lively, highly illustrated games and activities.

Round-up is especially designed for different students studying English in different ways.

It can be used:

- in class with a coursebook. Students do both oral work – in pairs and in groups – and written work in Round-up.
- after class. The "write-in" activities are ideal for homework. Students can practise what they have learned in the classroom.
- in the holidays for revision. Round-up has clear instructions and simple grammar boxes, so students can study at home without a teacher.

The Round-up Teacher's Guide includes a full answer key and four tests plus answer keys.

Pearson Education Limited
Edinburgh Gate, Harlow
Essex CM20 2JE England
And associated Companies throughout the world.

www.longman.com

First published in 1993 by E. Vlachou – "Express Publications".
First published by Longman Group Limited 1995.
This edition published by Pearson Education Limited 2003.
Twelfth impression 2009

Printed in China
CTPSC/12

Illustrated by Chris Zmertis and Terry Wilson.

ISBN 978-0-582-82341-9

1. Plurals of Countable and Uncountable Nouns

A Countable nouns are nouns which can be counted. They take "s" in the plural.

bananas dogs
cats books

1 Fill in the plural as in the example:

1. an orange - two *oranges* ..
2. a dog - three ....
3. a bat - two ....

B Nouns ending in -s, -ss, -sh, -ch, -x, -o take "-es" in the plural.

bus - buses	hairbrush - hairbrushes	box - boxes
dress - dresses	watch - watches	tomato - tomatoes

BUT

radio - radios piano - pianos photo - photos video - videos

2 Fill in the plural as in the example:

1. a torch - two *torches* ...
2. a glass - three ....
3. a fox - two ....

C Nouns ending in a consonant + y ➡ ies — baby - babies
Nouns ending in a vowel (a, e, o, u) +y ➡ ys — toy - toys

3 Fill in the plural as in the example:

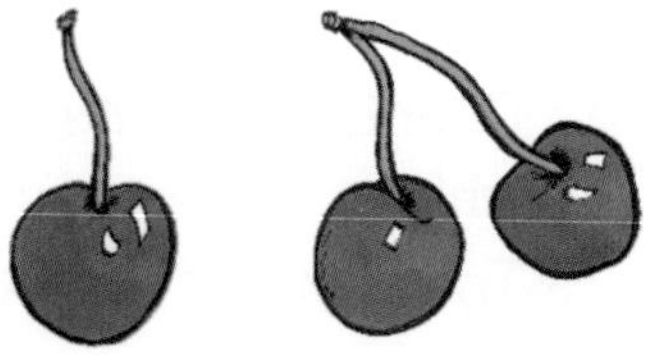

1. a lady - two .. *ladies* .. 2. a key - two .... 3. a cherry - two ....

D **Nouns ending in -f, -fe ⇨ ves leaf - leaves, wife - wives**

BUT

roof - roofs, chief - chiefs, handkerchief - handkerchiefs, proof - proofs

4 Fill in the plural as in the example:

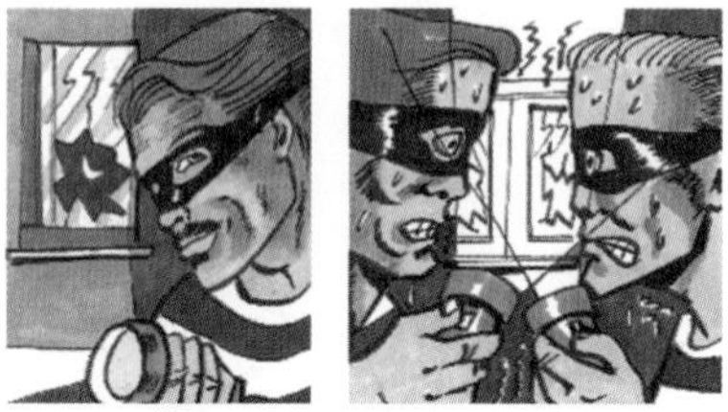

1. a thief - two .. *thieves* .. 2. a knife - two .... 3. a leaf - two ....

Pronunciation

/f/, /k/, /p/, /t/, /θ/		/s/, /ʃ/, /tʃ/, /dʒ/, /z/, /ʒ/		after other sounds	
/s/		/ɪz/		/z/	
cliffs	lollipops	foxes	bridges	pens	meals
proofs	spots	brushes	roses	babies	records
books	baths	churches	mirages	songs	rooms

5 Put the nouns in the correct list in the plural and read them out:

class, beach, boy, cat, cup, desk, roof, girl, potato, fork, shirt, pen, leaf, nose, bus, lemon, peach, box

/s/		/ɪz/		/z/	
.... *cats* ..	....	....	....	....	....
....	....	....	....	....	....
....	....	....	....	....	....

E **Irregular Plurals**

child - children	foot - feet	fish - fish	mouse - mice
man - men	tooth - teeth	sheep - sheep	ox - oxen
woman - women	goose - geese	deer - deer	louse - lice

6 Fill in the plural as in the example:

1. a girl - two . *girls* .....
2. a deer - two ....
3. a mouse - two ....

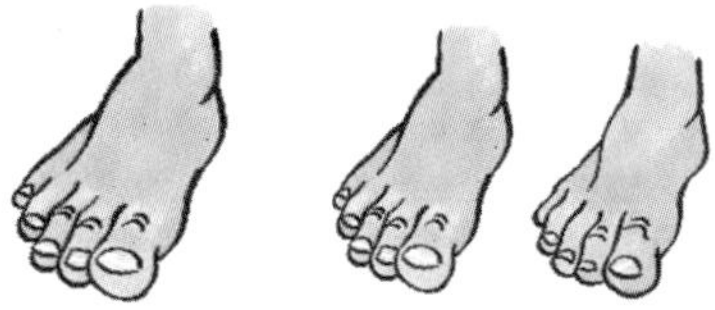

4. a bus - two ....
5. a foot - two ....
6. a snail - two ....

7. a sandwich - two ....
8. a butterfly - two ....
9. a wolf - two ....

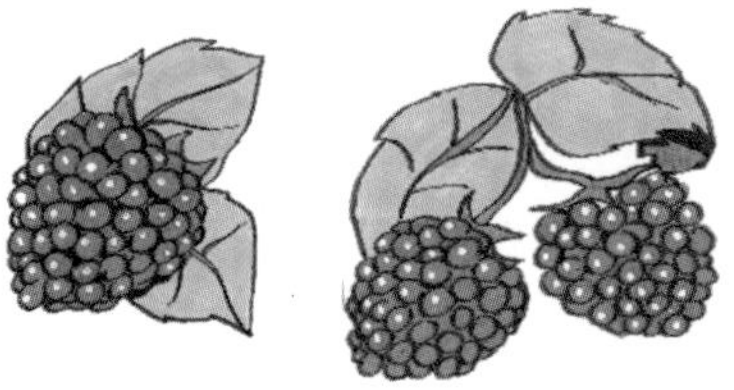

10. a lizard - two ....
11. a raspberry - two ....
12. a woman - two ....

7 Write the words in the plural and in the correct column.

radio, tomato, lady, boy, bench, teacher, watch, day, fox, loaf, handkerchief, kiss, fly, housewife, leaf, body, shelf, school, address, life, country, strawberry, baby, toy, half

- s	- es	- ies	- ves
..... *radios,*	....	....	....
....	....	....	....
....	....	....	....
....	....	....	....
....	....	....	....
....	....	....	....

F **Some nouns are uncountable. They have no plural. "A / an" is not used with uncountable nouns. "Some" is used with them. These nouns include:**

food :	butter, bread, meat, cheese, water, tea, coffee, wine, beer, milk, lemonade, chocolate, salt, pepper, fish etc.
material :	paper, wood, silver, gold, iron etc.
abstract nouns :	peace, anger, love etc.
many others :	money, snow, soap, furniture, petrol, oil, information, news etc.

8 Fill in the blanks with "a" or "some".

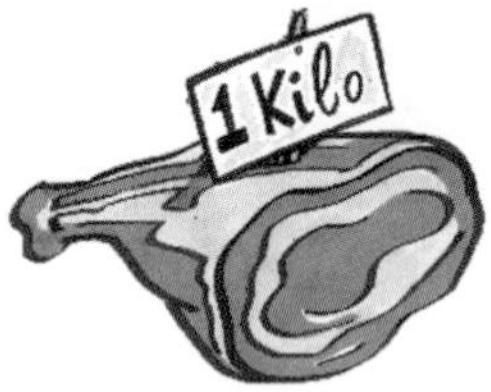

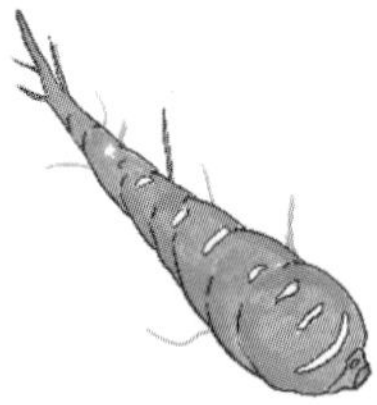

1. ... *some*.... meat 2. .... camera 3. .... soap 4. .... carrot

5. .... ring 6. .... rice 7. .... cheese 8. .... kangaroo

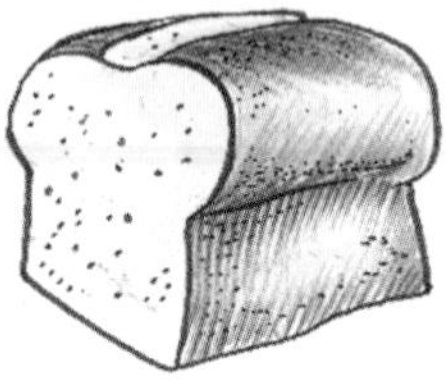

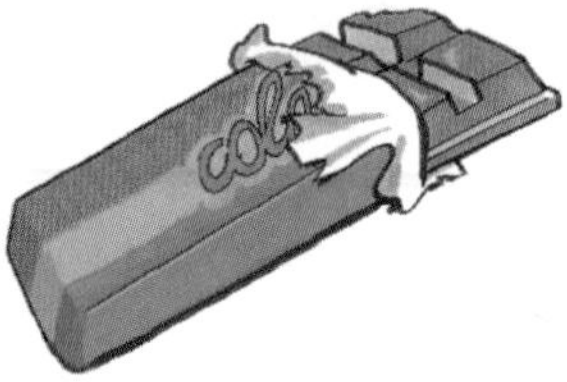

9. .... bread 10. .... money 11. .... goose 12. .... chocolate

Some is also used with countable nouns in the plural. **I've got some eggs.**

9 Fill in the blanks with "a", "an" or "some".

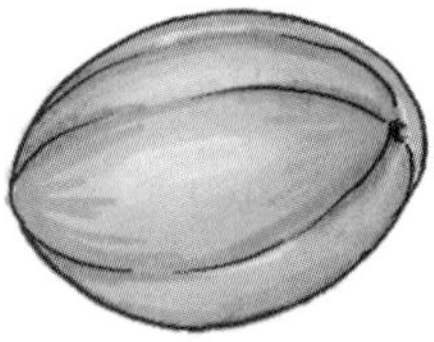

1. .. *some*... flowers 2. .... beer 3. .... melon 4. .... peach

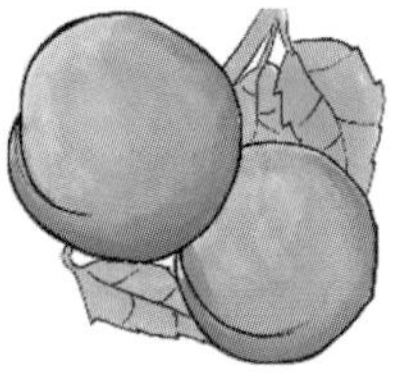

5. .... peaches 6. .... milk 7. .... orange 8. .... oranges

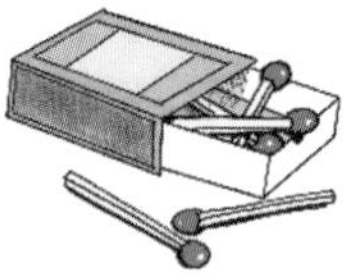

9. .... matches 10. .... T-shirt 11. .... grapes 12. .... sugar

G Some uncountable nouns can be made countable by using these words:

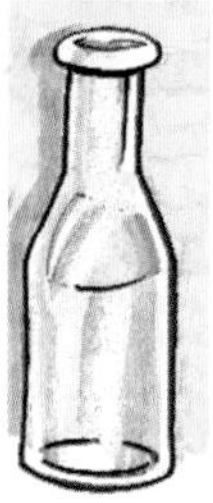

a bottle of milk

a glass of water

a jug of water

a cup of tea

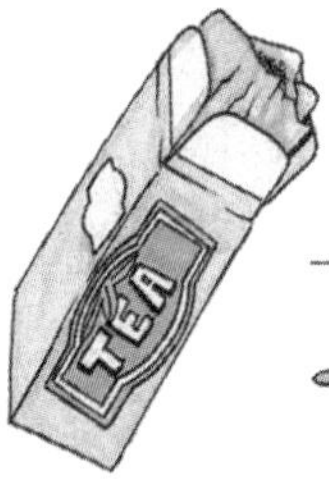

a packet of tea

a jar of honey

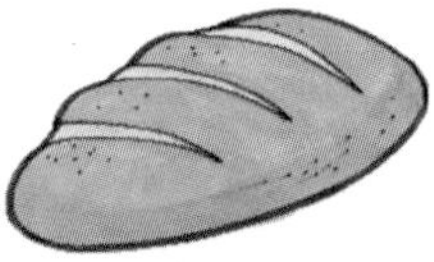

a loaf of bread

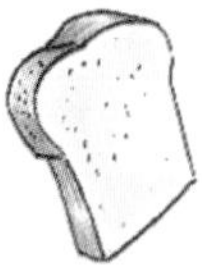

a slice of bread

a carton of milk

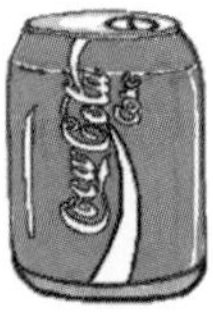

a can of Coke

a bottle of Coke

a bowl of sugar

a kilo of meat

a bar of soap

a bar of chocolate

a piece of chocolate

a piece of cheese

a piece of furniture

10 Fill in the plural as in the example:

1. Some Coke.Two .*cans / bottles of Coke* .
2. A fish. Three ....
3. A room. Five ....
4. Some jam. Two ....
5. Some soap. Three..................................
6. Some lemonade. Two ....
7. A spoon. Three ....
8. A flower. Two ....
9. Some paper. Three ....
10. Some tea. Two ....
11. A table.Two ....
12. Some bread.Two ....
13. A skirt. Three ....
14. Some water. Two ....
15. An egg. Four ....
16. Some cheese. Two ....
17. Some milk. Three ....
18. A man. Two ....
19. A mouse. Three ....
20. Some coffee. Two ....

H **Adjectives take no "-s" in the plural. ➡ a new record - two new records**

11 Fill in the plural as in the example :

1. A chair. Four ..... *chairs* ....
2. An old lady. Two ....
3. Some chocolate. Two ....
4. Some honey. Three ....
5. A tall boy. Two ....
6. A pretty butterfly. Three ....
7. A clever student. Ten..................................
8. A heavy suitcase. Two ....
9. Some meat. Two..................................
10. A new hat. Two ....
11. A famous actress. Two..................................
12. A goose. Ten ....

Oral Activity 1

The teacher divides the class into two teams and says nouns in the singular. The teams in turn say the plural of each word. Each correct answer gets 1 point. The team with the most points is the winner.

Teacher :	pencil
Team A S1 :	pencils
Teacher :	tooth
Team B S1 :	teeth

Teacher :	sheep
Team A S2 :	sheeps
Teacher :	Wrong! sheep. Group A doesn't get a point.

Writing Activity 1

The teacher asks the students to look around the classroom and write, in only 5 minutes, how many things or people they can see.

e.g. four walls, two pictures, eight boys etc.

2. Personal Pronouns / Be / Have (got) / Can

A man or a boy is "he".

Look at him!
He is a waiter.

Singular	Plural	Singular	Plural
before verbs as subjects		after verbs as objects	
I	We	Me	Us
You	You	You	You
He	They	Him	Them
She		Her	
It		It	

A woman or a girl is "she".

Look at her!
She is a doctor.

A thing or an animal is "it" but a pet can be "he / she".

Look at it!
It is a book.

Look at it! It is a peacock.

Look at her!
She is Daisy.

12 Write "he", "she", "it" or "they".

1. ..... *it* ....

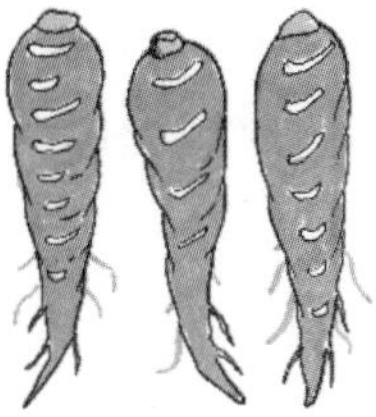

2. ....

3. ....

4. ....

5. ....

6. ....

7. ....

8. ....

13 Fill in "he", "she", "it", "we", "you" or "they" as in the example :

1. table .... *it* ....
2. You and Mark ....
3. John and I ....
4. Helen and Mary ....
5. flowers ....
6. Grandfather and I..............
7. brother ....
8. sister ....
9. girl ....
10. trees ....
11. shops ....
12. lion ....

Oral Activity 2

The teacher divides the class into two teams. Play the game as follows:

Teacher : Ann
Team A S1 : she
Teacher : Tony
Team B S1 : he

Teacher : Peter and I
Team A S2 : they
Teacher : Wrong! We.
Team A doesn't get a point.

Each correct answer gets 1 point. The team with the most points is the winner.

The Verb "to be"

Affirmative		Negative		Interrogative
Long form	**Short form**	**Long form**	**Short form**	
I am	I'm	I am not	I'm not	Am I?
You are	You're	You are not	You aren't	Are you?
He is	He's	He is not	He isn't	Is he?
She is	She's	She is not	She isn't	Is she?
It is	It's	It is not	It isn't	Is it?
We are	We're	We are not	We aren't	Are we?
You are	You're	You are not	You aren't	Are you?
They are	They're	They are not	They aren't	Are they?

14 Fill in as in the example :

Long form

1. She .. *is* .... at school.
2. You .... not a teacher.
3. It .... a bird.
4. I .... not old.
5. We .... from Italy.

Short form

She.. *'s* .... at school.
You .... a teacher.
It .... a bird.
I .... old.
We .... from Italy.

Short answers

Am **I tall?**	**Yes, I** am.	**No, I'm** not.
Is **he / she / it in the bedroom?**	**Yes, he / she / it** is.	**No, he / she / it** isn't.
Are **we / you / they doctors?**	**Yes, we / you / they** are.	**No, we / you / they** aren't.

15 Fill in the blanks and answer the questions as in the example :

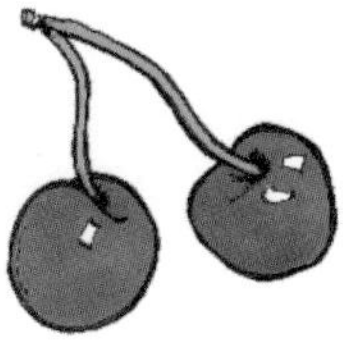

1. Look at ...... *them* ...!
Are they strawberries?
....*No, they aren't*. .
....*They're* .. cherries.

2. Look at ....!
.... a cook?
....
.... a waiter.

3. Look at ....!
.... a robot?
....
.... a robot.

4. Look at ....!
.... balls?
....
.... balloons.

5. Look at ....!
.... horses?
....
.... donkeys.

6. Look at ....!
.... a doctor?
....
.... a doctor.

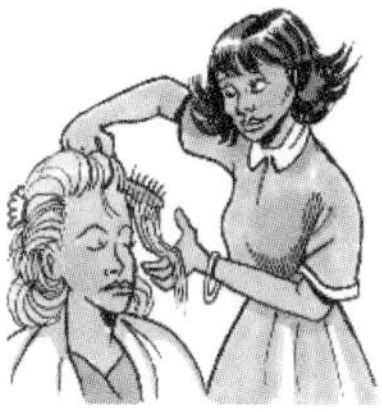

7. Look at ....!
.... I a teacher?
....
.... a hairdresser.

8. Look at ....!
.... we policemen?
....
.... tennis players.

The Verb "to have (got)"

Affirmative		Negative		Interrogative
Long form	**Short form**	**Long form**	**Short form**	
I have got	I've got	I have not got	I haven't got	Have I got?
You have got	You've got	You have not got	You haven't got	Have you got?
He has got	He's got	He has not got	He hasn't got	Has he got?
She has got	She's got	She has not got	She hasn't got	Has she got?
It has got	It's got	It has not got	It hasn't got	Has it got?
We have got	We've got	We have not got	We haven't got	Have we got?
You have got	You've got	You have not got	You haven't got	Have you got?
They have got	They've got	They have not got	They haven't got	Have they got?

16 Fill in the blanks as in the example :

Long form	Short form
I .. *have got* .... a walkman.	I ..*'ve got* .... a walkman.

1. John .... black hair.	John .... black hair.
2. We .... not .... a boat.	We .... a boat.
3. They .... a garden.	They .... a garden.
4. You .... blue eyes.	You .... blue eyes.
5. He .... not .... a pen.	He .... a pen.
6. She .... a car.	She .... a car.

Short answers

Have you got a pen?	**Yes, I / we have.**	**No, I / we haven't.**
Has he / she / it got a pen?	**Yes, he / she / it has.**	**No, he / she / it hasn't.**
Have we / you / they got a pen?	**Yes, we / you / they have.**	**No, we / you / they haven't.**

17 Ask and answer as in the example :

1. he / small ears?
..*Has he got small*..
.*ears? No, he hasn't.*
He's got big ears....

2. they / tails?
....
....
....

3. it / legs?
....
....
....

4. she / red hair?
....
....
....

5. they / radio?
....
....
....

6. he / hat?
....
....
....

18 Fill in the blanks as in the example :

1. I ... *am* .... Jane.
.*I am* ..a dressmaker.
.*I have got* ..a sewing machine.

2. She .... Ann.
... a business woman.
.... a computer.

3. They .... Jim and Chris.
.... students.
.... books.

4. He .... Tom.
.... a doctor.
.... a stethoscope.

5. We .... Ben and Anna.
.... farmers.
.... a tractor.

6. He .... Bob.
.... a waiter.
.... a tray.

Oral Activity 3

The teacher divides the class into two teams. Students look at Ex. 18 in their books. Then team B closes books. Students from team A make true or false statements. Students from team B give the correct responses. The team gets 1 point for each correct response. Play the game twice and change the roles of the teams. The team that gets the most points is the winner.

Team A S1 : Jane is a doctor. She's got a stethoscope.
Team B S1 : False! Jane isn't a doctor. She hasn't got a stethoscope. Jane is a dressmaker. She's got a sewing machine. (1 point for team B)
Team A S2 : Ben and Anna are astronauts. They've got spacesuits.
Team B S2 : True! Ben and Anna are astronauts. They've got spacesuits.
Teacher : Wrong! Team B doesn't get a point. (1 point for team A) etc.

Writing Activity 2

In only 5 minutes, write about yourself and your friends.

e.g. I am Tom. I am a student. He is Nick. He is a student. etc.

The Verb "Can"

Affirmative	Negative		Interrogative
	Long form	**Short form**	
I can	I cannot	I can't	Can I?
You can	You cannot	You can't	Can you?
He can	He cannot	He can't	Can he?
She can	She cannot	She can't	Can she?
It can	It cannot	It can't	Can it?
We can	We cannot	We can't	Can we?
You can	You cannot	You can't	Can you?
They can	They cannot	They can't	Can they?

Short answers

Can you swim?	Yes, I can.	No, I can't.

19 Ask and answer as in the example :

	use a computer	cook	type	ski
George	✓		✓	
Jenny		✓		✓
Laura & Emma	✓	✓	✓	
You				

1. ..*Can George use a computer? Yes, he can. Can he cook? No, he can't. Can he type?*... ...*Yes, he can. Can he ski? No, he can't. So George can use a computer and type* .... *but he can't cook or ski.*..............................
2. ....
3. ....
4. ....

20 Ask and answer as in the example :

1. (write) ....*Can she write?*... .... *No, she can't.* .....
2. (run fast) ....
3. (fly) ....

4. (play tennis) ....

5. (walk) ....

6. (jump) ....

21 Fill in the spaces then write sentences about yourself.

Attach your photo here

Name :	....	...I'm..................
Nationality :	....	....
Job :	....	....
Hair :	....	....
Eyes :	....	....
Abilities :	....	....

Oral Activity 4 Guessing Game 1

The teacher divides the class into two teams. The teacher writes a list of ten verbs on the board before the game starts. Then he / she asks one student (the leader) to come to the front of the class. The teacher whispers one of the verbs e.g. "dance" into his / her ear. By asking questions, the students try to guess what he / she can do. The team which finds out wins.

write, draw, dance, sing, play tennis, jump, drive a car, ride a horse, swim, run fast

Team A S1 : Can you jump?
Leader : No, I can't.
Team B S1 : Can you play tennis?
Leader : No, I can't.

Team A S2 : Can you drive a car?
Leader : No, I can't.
Team B S2 : Can you dance?
Leader : Yes, I can.

Team B gets 1 point. The teacher chooses another leader and the class plays the game again.

Writing Activity 3

In only 5 minutes, write down as many things as possible that you can or can't do.

3. Possessives / Demonstratives

This isn't my T-shirt. It's your T-shirt. That T-shirt is mine.
This T-shirt isn't mine. It is yours. That's my T-shirt.

Personal pronouns		Possessive adjectives	Possessive pronouns
before verbs as subjects	after verbs as objects	followed by nouns	not followed by nouns
I	Me	My	Mine
You	You	Your	Yours
He / She / It	Him / Her / It	His / Her / Its	His / Hers / –
We	Us	Our	Ours
You	You	Your	Yours
They	Them	Their	Theirs

Possessive case with people

We use 's with one person.
Jane's umbrella

We use s' with two or more people . . .
the cooks' hats

BUT... we use 's with irregular plurals.
the men's ties

We also use 's with animals.
the dog's food

Possessive case with things

We use "of" with things

the floor of the bathroom

22 Look at the pictures and write as in the example :

1. I've got .... a handkerchief.
   It's ... my .... handkerchief.

2. He .... a calculator.
   It's .... calculator.

3. She .... a mask.
   It's .... mask.

4. They .... a motorcycle.
   It's .... motorcycle.

5. We .... hats.
   They're .... hats.

6. You .... a scarf.
   It's .... scarf.

23 Fill in "it's", "its", "they're" or "their".

John and Mary have got a house in the country. 1) .... Their .... house is big. It has got five rooms. 2) .... rooms are big too. Paul and Liz are John and Mary's friends. 3) .... 4) .... friends. They have got a dog. 5) .... a small white dog. 6) .... name is Prince.

24 Underline the correct word, then explain in your mother tongue.

1. My (friend's, friends') name is Mike.
2. His (cousin's, cousins') names are Jean and Chris.
3. Our (children's, childrens') names are Catherine and Paula.
4. My (brother's, brothers') name is Mark.
5. My (brother's, brothers') names are Ben and Tom.
6. This is the (lady's, ladies') dress.
7. Look at the (house's roof, roof of the house).

25 Look at the pictures and write as in the example :

Kristi

gloves

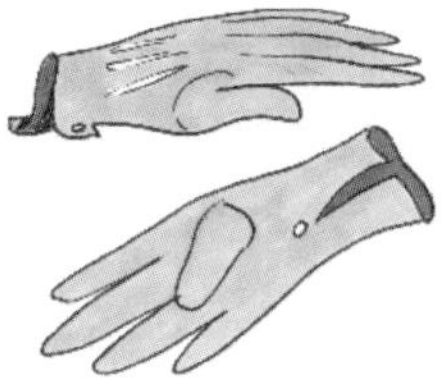

1. These are ..... Kristi's .
   ...... gloves. ....
   They're ..... her gloves..
   These ..... gloves are ..
   .... hers. .....

Ted  socks 

2. These are ....
   They're ....
   These ....

the boys  pencils 

3. These are ....
   They're ....
   These ....

Mother  apron 

4. This is ....
   It's ....
   This ....

the peacock  tail 

5. This is ....
   It's ....

the roof 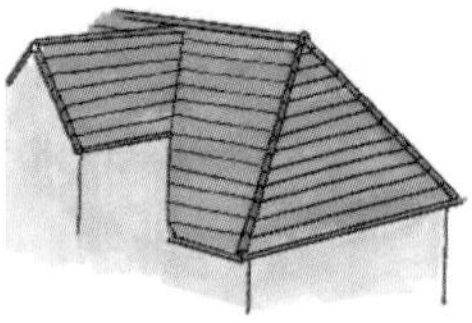 house 

6. This is ....
   It's ....

26 First say then write as in the example :

	food	sport	singer	colour	actor or actress
Andrew	spaghetti	golf	Madonna	white	Kim Basinger
Carol	chicken	swimming	Michael Jackson	red	Robert Redford
Bob & Mary	fish & chips	basketball	Elton John	blue	Liz Taylor

1. . *Andrew's favourite food is spaghetti. His favourite sport is golf. His favourite singer* .. *is Madonna. His favourite colour is white. His favourite actress is Kim Basinger.*.....
2. ....
   ....
   ....
   ....
3. ....
   ....

....

....

4. My favourite food is ....

....

....

....

27 Circle the possessives and underline the short forms.

Look! This is Johnny Rock. He's a famous pop star. Johnny's group's name's "The Rockers". This is the Rockers' new album. It's called "Funky". And look at Johnny. He's got long green hair. Dave's hair is red but Ringo's bald!

28 Underline the correct word as in the example :

1. Mark is (their, theirs) cousin.
2. This is our car. It's (our, ours).
3. These are Mary's books.
   They're (her, hers).
4. Blue is (my, mine) favourite colour.
5. You can't have this book. It isn't (your, yours).
6. (Her, Hers) house is big.
7. Is this (your, yours) coat? No, it isn't (my, mine).
8. Are these pens Liz and Bob's?
   Yes, they're (their, theirs).
9. This is Father's car. It's (his, hers).
10. That is (our, ours) house. It's (our, ours).

This - These (Near)	That - Those (Far)
 **This** pigeon  **These** pigeons	 **That** pigeon  **Those** pigeons

29 Fill in "This", "These", "That" or "Those".

1. ..... That ....is a grasshopper.  

2. .... is a bee.  

3. .... are swans. 

4. .... are caterpillars.  

5. .... is a cockroach. 

6. .... are ladybirds.  

Oral Activity 5

The teacher divides the class into two teams. Then, in turn, students point to various objects in the class and make sentences using **this - these - that - those**. Each correct sentence gets 1 point. When a student does not produce a correct sentence his/her team doesn't get a point. The group with the most points is the winner.

Team A S1 :	This is a desk.	Team A S2 :	This is chairs.
Team B S1 :	That is a chair.	Teacher :	Wrong! These are chairs. Team A doesn't get a point.

4. Articles

The Indefinite Article "A" - "An"

a + consonant sound		an + vowel sound (a,e,i,o,u)	

a judge	a detective	an artist	an astronaut

We use "a" before "u" when we pronounce it with a "y" sound. a uniform BUT an umbrella
We use "an" before "h" when it is silent. an hour BUT a horse

30 Fill in "a" or "an".

1. .... a .... guitar 2. .... accordion 3. .... violin 4. .... organ

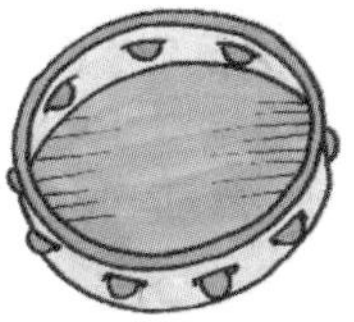

5. ....piano 6. .... drum 7. .... harp 8. .... tambourine

Oral Activity 6 - Memory Game

First make sure you know all the words in the picture. Then look at the picture for 1 minute. Finally, close your book and name as many things or people as possible using "a" / "an". Play the memory game in teams. The winning team is the one which remembers the most things.

The Definite Article "The"

The / ðə / + consonant sound		The / ðɪ/ + vowel sound (a,e,i,o,u)	

the **lobster**	the **prawn**	the **octopus**	the **oyster**

31 Put the nouns in the correct column according to the way "the" is said.

apple, baby, orange, office, meat, wine, woman, animal, money, egg, dress, eye

The / ðə /		The / ðɪ /	
..... *baby*	....	....	....
....	....	....	....
....	....	....	....

We use "a / an" :	We use "the" :
1. **with singular countable nouns when we are talking about them in general.** **An** elephant is **a** big animal. (Which elephant? We don't mean a specific elephant; we mean elephants in general.)	1. **with singular or plural nouns when we are talking about something specific which we either already know about or when the noun is mentioned for a second time.** **The** car in front of **the** house is Ted's. (Which car? Not any car. **The** car which is in front of the house.)
2. **after the verbs "to be" and "to have".** He's **an** astronaut. He's got **a** pet cat.	2. **with nouns which are unique.** **The sun** is shining. (= There's only one sun.) **The Acropolis** is in Athens.
We don't use "a / an" :	**We don't use "the" :**
with uncountable or plural nouns. We can use some or no article instead. I want some **sugar** and some **strawberries**. I don't like **apples**.	**with proper nouns or possessive adjectives.** **Emma** is from **London**. **Her** father is from **Leeds**. **BUT family and nationality names take "the".** **The** Browns, **The** Germans

32 First read out the words then fill in the blanks with "a", "an" or "some".

1. .... *some* ......tea	6. .... hour	11. .... salt	16. .... pepper
2. .... elephant	7. .... cup	12. ....eye	17. .... horse
3. .... box	8. .... egg	13. .... uncle	18. .... water
4. .... house	9. .... union	14. .... blouse	19. .... money
5. .... onions	10. .... plates	15. .... farmers	20. .... milk

33 Fill in "a", "an" or "the".

Tina : Are these Mother's things?

Father: What are they?

Tina: 1) ... *A* ... hat, 2) .... orange dress, 3) .... coat and 4) .... pair of glasses.

Father : 5) .... hat and 6) .... coat are mine. 7) .... orange dress and 8) .... pair of glasses are your mother's.

34 Fill in "a", "an" or "the".

Assistant : Here you are. 1) ..... *A* .... stamp, 2) .... envelope, 3) .... pen and 4) .... notebook.

Mr Black : Oh, 5) .... envelope is too big and 6) .... pen isn't blue, it's red. Can I have 7) .... small envelope and 8) .... blue pen, please?

35 Fill in "a", "an" or "the" where necessary.

1. This is .... *an* .... egg.
2. Where is .... post office?
3. .... Lucy's uncle is .... teacher.
4. Julie has got .... orange.
5. This is .... way to school.
6. It's .... long way to .... office.
7. There are a lot of flowers in .... garden.
8. .... Italians like .... spaghetti.
9. ....white hat is Mother's.
10. .... Peter and .... Ben are brothers.
11. .... Eiffel Tower is in Paris.
12. .... Sphinx is in .... Egypt.
13. There's some sugar in .... bowl.
14. Open .... door, please!
15. These are .... our shoes.
16. .... bottle of beer, please!

17. .... Smiths have four children.
18. .... English like .... tea.
19. .... small black dog is mine.
20. .... her eyes are brown.
21. .... snakes are dangerous.
22. .... woman in the green dress is Mary.

36 Fill in "a", "an" or "the" where necessary.

1) ...✗.... Mrs Jones has 2) .... new office. It has 3) .... desk, 4) .... telephone and 5) .... expensive computer. 6) .... Mrs Jones is on 7) .... phone now and her secretary is at 8) .... computer. 9) .... Mrs Jones and 10) .... her secretary are very busy in 11) .... office today.

37 Fill in "a", "an" or "the" where necessary.

There is 1) ... a .... swing,2) .... tree, 3) .... old bicycle, 4) .... cat, 5) .... angry dog and 6) .... bird. Sally is on 7) .... swing, 8) .... Tom and 9) .... Pat are in 10) .... tree. 11) .... angry dog is at 12) .... bottom of 13) .... tree and 14) .... cat is on 15) .... branch! The bird is on the seat of 16) .... old bicycle. It's 17) .... Sunday and 18) .... Browns are in the garden. They are not in 19) .... office today.

Oral Activity 7

Look at "Oral Activity 6" on p. 21 and play the memory game using "the".

Revision Exercises I

38 Choose the correct item.

1. This is .... B .... teacher.
   A) we B) our C) ours
2. Claire is from .... Paris.
   A) ... B) the C) a
3. These are .... pencils.
   A) of Ann's B) Anns' C) Ann's
4. The children .... in the garden.
   A) is B) are C) am
5. Those shoes are ....
   A) mine B) my C) me
6. There's .... man at the door.
   A) the B) some C) a
7. Look at .... ! She's a singer.
   A) hers B) she C) her
8. I can see two ....
   A) baby B) babys C) babies
9. This is the .... bag.
   A) lady's B) ladies's C) ladys'
10. There's a .... of bread on the table.
    A) bar B) loaf C) carton
11. Paul is .... brother.
    A) theirs B) their C) them
12. There are stars in .... sky.
    A) a B) an C) the

39 Find the mistake and correct it.

1. I've got two ~~knifes~~. .... knives ....
2. This is a jug of jam. ....
3. There's a beer in the glass. ....
4. There are mouses in the house. ....
5. He's got a umbrella. ....
6. My fathers' name is John. ....
7. There's a butter in the fridge. ....
8. This is Ann's pen. It's her. ....

40 Fill in "a", "an" or "the".

Sally: In our house we've got 1) .. a .. TV, 2) .... fridge, 3) .... electric cooker and 4) ...... radio.
John: Are they all yours?
Sally: 5) ..... radio is mine but 6) ...... electric cooker, 7) ...... fridge and 8) .... TV are my parents'.

41 Fill in the plural.

1. Some soap. Two ... bars of soap ....
2. A donkey. Two ....
3. A tall fireman. Two ....
4. One tooth. Two ....
5. Some furniture. Two ....
6. A housewife. Two ....

42 Write about these people.

	George	Pam	Peter & John	You
Nationality	Italian	English	Irish	
Job	teacher	student	doctors	
Hair	brown	red	black	
Eyes	brown	blue	green	
Abilities	dance, swim	ride, sing	drive, play tennis	

1. George ...... *is Italian. He's a teacher. He's got brown hair and brown eyes.* .... *He can dance and swim.* ....
2. Pam ....
3. Peter and John ....
4. I ....

43 Fill in "his", "her", "its", "she", "they" or "their".

This is Mrs Adams. 1) .... *She* .... is married. 2) .... husband's name is Peter. 3) .... have two children. 4) .... names are Jim and Gina. Jim's got a pet dog. 5) .... name is Blanko. 6) .... all live in a big house on Green Road. 7) .... house is nice and big. 8) .... garden has got a lot of flowers. Mrs Adams loves 9) .... garden. She often sits outside and reads 10) .... book. Peter usually smokes 11) .... pipe outside too. Jim likes playing with 12) .... dog in the garden but Gina often pulls 13) .... tail. 14) .... is a bad girl.

44 Underline the correct item.

1. This is the (<u>children's</u>, childrens') room.
2. These are the (boy's, boys') families.
3. These are the (tree's leaves, leaves of the tree).
4. That's (Mum's, Mums') dress.
5. This is (John's, Johns') book.
6. Those are the (ladys', lady's) shoes.

5. Expressing Quantity

Have you got many books in your bag, John?

No, I haven't got many books. I've got a few books and a lot of sweets.

Have you got much money in your pockets?

Er ... no, I haven't got much money. I've got a little money and a lot of chocolate.

	countables	uncountables
Positive	a lot of / lots of	a lot of / lots of
Interrogative	many	much
Negative	many	much
Positive	(a) few	(a) little

a few cherries

few cherries

a little cheese

little cheese

1. A lot of or lots of are used in the affirmative with countables or uncountables:
There are **a lot of / lots of** stars in the sky.
There's **a lot of / lots of** milk in the bottle.

2. Many (with countables) and much (with uncountables) are used in questions and negations. Many and much can also be used in the affirmative in formal English:
How **many** friends have you got?
There isn't **much** cheese in the fridge.
Many people can't find jobs nowadays.

3. Many and much are used after so:
There are **so many** children in the room that there's no place to sit.

4. A few (with countables) / A little (with uncountables) mean 'some' (but not much); (very) few / (very) little mean 'not enough':
I need **a few** eggs and **a little** butter to make a cake.
There are **very few** eggs and there is **very little** butter. We need to buy some.

45 Fill in "much" or "many".

1. How ...... *much* ...... wine?
2. How .... children?
3. How .... shops?
4. How .... pencils?
5. How .... water?
6. How .... glasses?
7. How .... records?
8. How .... bread?
9. How .... tea?

46 Fill in "much", "many" or "a lot of".

1. There aren't .... *many* .... mushrooms.

2. There aren't .... radishes.

3. There isn't .... honey.

4. There are .... blueberries.

5. There's .... jam.

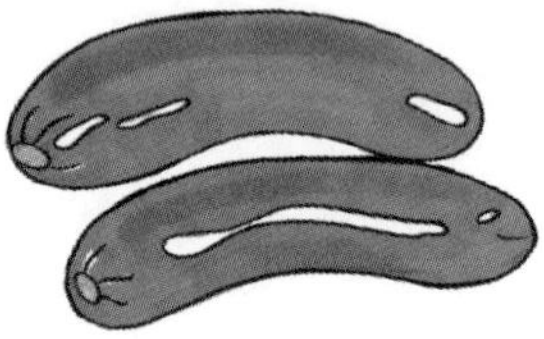

6. There aren't .... sausages.

47 Fill in the blanks with "much", "many" or "a lot of".

1. There are so .... *many* ...... birds in the sky!
2. I haven't got .... homework today.
3. John hasn't got .... money.
4. There aren't .... cars in the street.
5. There is .... gold in the bag.
6. Are there .... apples on the tree?
7. Jane spends .... money at the shops.
8. Have you got .... bread in the cupboard?
9. Are there .... children on the beach?
10. We are early. We have .... time.

48 Fill in "few", "a few", "little" or "a little".

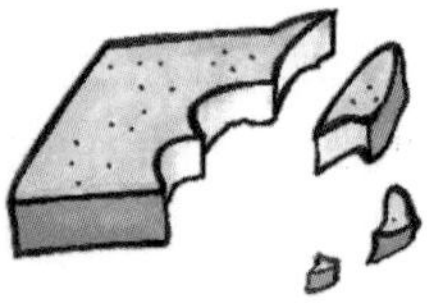

1. There's ... *little* ...... bread.

2. There are .... grapes.

3. There are .... pears.

4. There's .... money. 5. There's .... money. 6. There are .... biscuits.

49 Choose the correct item.

1. Have you got .... A .... friends?
   A) many B) much C) a lot of
2. There are .... people in the room.
   A) much B) a little C) a lot of
3. Can I have .... sugar, please?
   A) a few B) a little C) little
4. How .... oranges are on the table?
   A) many B) a few C) much
5. How .... money has Fred got?
   A) many B) little C) much
6. There are .... monkeys at the zoo.
   A) much B) a few C) a little
7. There are .... chairs in the room.
   A) a little B) much C) a few
8. We are late. We have very .... time!
   A) little B) few C) many

Interrogative	Positive	Negative
Any	**Some**	**No / not any**
Are there **any** eggs?	Yes, there are **some** eggs.	No, there are **no** eggs. No, there are**n't any** eggs.

1. **"Some" is used in positive statements, "any" in questions and "no" or "not any" in negations.**
   Is there **any** meat in the fridge? No, there's **no** meat in the fridge. or There is**n't any** meat in the fridge. There are **some** eggs.

2. **"Some" is also used in the interrogative when we expect a "Yes" answer or when we want to make an offer.**
   Would you like **some** tea? Can I have **some** coffee, please?

3. **"Any" is also used in positive statements but it means "It doesn't matter which".**
   Which book should I get? Get **any** book you would like to read!

50 Fill in "some" or "any".

Stephanie is packing her suitcase.
I need 1) .... *some* .... shoes. I don't need to take 2) .... boots. I need 3) .... dresses and 4) .... blouses. I don't need 5) .... jumpers or gloves. I don't need 6) .... warm clothes at all. I need 7) .... jeans and I need 8) .... money of course.

51 Look at the picture and write sentences as in the example:

1. chairs? . *Are there any chairs?* ....
   ....*Yes, there are some chairs* ....
2. cats? ....
   ....
3. children? ....
   ....
4. fish? ....
   ....
5. flowers? ....
   ....
6. milk? ....
   ....
7. butter? ....
   ....
8. dogs? ....
   ....
9. bread? ....
   ....

52 Fill in "some", "any", "how much" or "how many".

Chris and Laura are making a shopping list.

Chris: Have we got 1) .... *any* .... bread?
Laura: Yes, we've got 2) ....
Chris: 3) .... bread have we got?
Laura: One loaf.
Chris: We haven't got 4) .... biscuits and there aren't 5) .... crisps. Shall we buy 6) ....?
Laura: OK. We'll get 7) .... biscuits and 8) .... crisps.
Chris: What about potatoes? Are there 9) .... potatoes?
Laura: Yes, there are 10) ....
Chris: Is there 11) .... rice?
Laura: No, there isn't 12) .... rice. We've got to buy 13) ....
Chris: 14) .... rice do we need?
Laura: Two packets.
Chris: Have we got 15) .... milk?
Laura: No, we've got to buy 16) ....
Chris: 17) .... cartons of milk?
Laura: Four cartons.

53 Fill in "a little" or "a few".

1. .... *a little* .... lemonade
2. .... men
3. .... milk
4. .... sweets
5. .... women
6. .... houses
7. .... money
8. .... friends
9. .... snow

	Positive	Interrogative	Negative
people	someone	anyone	no one / not anyone
	somebody	anybody	nobody / not anybody
things	something	anything	nothing / not anything
place	somewhere	anywhere	nowhere / not anywhere

The compounds "someone / anyone" etc follow the same rules as "any" and "some".

Is there **anybody** in the kitchen? Yes, there is **somebody** in the kitchen but there is **nobody** in the bedroom and there is**n't anybody** in the sitting room either.

54 Fill in the blanks with "someone", "anyone", "somewhere", "anywhere" or "nothing".

Do you know 1) .. *anywhere* .. nice to go on holiday? I want to go 2)............... hot where I can do 3) .... all day but lie on the beach. I know 4) .... in Italy and he says there isn't 5) .... better. He knows a lot of countries because he travels everywhere for his job. I want to go to Spain but I don't know 6) .... there. 7) .... must know a good place to go to!

55 Look at the picture and fill in "someone", "no one" or "anyone".

There is 1) .... *no one* ... on the roof of the house. There's 2) .... at the door. There isn't 3) .... near the gate. There is 4) .... on the swing. There is 5) .... behind the tree. There isn't 6) .... near the window. There's 7) .... near the cat. There's 8) .... in the tree.

56 Look at the picture and fill in "something", "anything" or "nothing".

There is 1) ..... *something* .... on the table. There is 2) .... on the chair. There is 3) .... on the cooker. There isn't 4) .... under the table. There's 5) .... in the cupboard. There's 6) .... on the wall. It's a clock. There's 7) .... in the basket. It's empty. There is 8) .... on the floor. It's a mouse.

Oral Activity 8

Look again at the pictures for Exercises 55 and 56. Ask and answer questions using anyone, anything, something, someone, no one or nothing.

Is there anyone on the roof of the house? No, there is no one on the roof of the house etc.

6. Present Simple

Do you know Patrick Rich? There he is! He usually drives a sports car! He doesn't like slow cars. He likes fast cars.

He sometimes drives too fast!
CRASH

We use Present Simple for permanent states or habitual actions.

Time Expressions used with Present Simple :			
every day in the afternoon often	every morning in the evening never	every year always rarely	at night usually sometimes etc.

Affirmative	Negative		Interrogative
	Long form	**Short form**	
I talk	I do not talk	I don't talk	Do I talk?
You talk	You do not talk	You don't talk	Do you talk?
He talks	He does not talk	He doesn't talk	Does he talk?
She talks	She does not talk	She doesn't talk	Does she talk?
It talks	It does not talk	It doesn't talk	Does it talk?
We talk	We do not talk	We don't talk	Do we talk?
You talk	You do not talk	You don't talk	Do you talk?
They talk	They do not talk	They don't talk	Do they talk?

Spelling

Verbs ending in -ss, -sh, -ch, -x, -o ➡ -es	Verbs ending in consonant + y ➡ -ies
I watch - he watches I go - he goes	I study - he studies **BUT verbs ending in a vowel (a,e,o,u)+y** ➡ ys I buy - he buys

57 Write the verbs in the third person singular.

1. I fly - it ..... *flies*..............
2. You run - he ....
3. We catch - she ....
4. I play - she ....
5. We hurry - he ....
6. You stay - she ....
7. I do - he ....
8. You see - he ....
9. They take - he ....

Pronunciation

58 Put the verbs in the correct column in the third person singular, then read them out.

work, play, come, watch, talk, dance, go, laugh, drive, smoke, kiss, sleep, swim, wash, mix, visit, close, know, ride, open, teach, speak, change, sit

/ s /		/ ɪz /		/ z /	
/f/, /k/, /p/, /t/		/s/, /ʃ/, /tʃ/, /dʒ/, /z/		after other sounds	
.*he works*..	....	*he washes*.	..*he swims*.	....	....
....	....	....	....	....	....
....	....	....	....	....	....
....	....	....	....	....	....

Adverbs of Frequency

Adverbs of Frequency go after the verbs "to be" and "can" but before the main verbs.

She	always often usually	reads books.
He is	sometimes seldom rarely never	late.

59 How often do they brush their teeth? Fill in an Adverb of Frequency.

He *always* brushes his teeth after meals.

She .... brushes her teeth.

They .... brush their teeth.

He .... brushes his teeth.

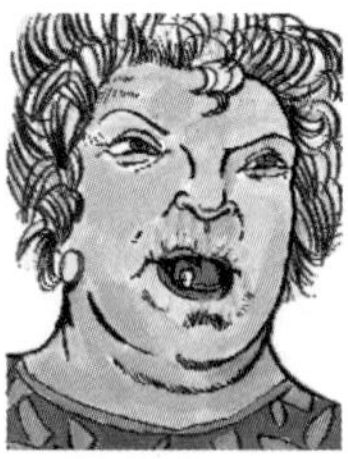

She .... brushes her teeth.

I .... brush my teeth.

60 Complete the sentences as in the example :

Long form	Short form
1. She ..... *does not* .... like apples.	She ...... *doesn't* .... like apples.
2. We .... work on Sunday.	We .... work on Sunday.
3. He .... help me.	He .... help me.
4. They .... drive fast.	They .... drive fast.
5. It .... fly.	It .... fly.

61 First write about James, Kim and Greg then about yourself.

	be late	drink tea	play tennis	watch TV	smoke
James	always	usually	often	rarely	never
Kim & Greg	never	always	sometimes	often	rarely
You					

1. James ..... *is always late. He usually drinks tea. He* ....

....

2. Kim & Greg ....

....

3. I ....

....

62 Look at Exercise 61 again and then ask and answer questions.

e.g. How often do Kim & Greg drink tea? They always drink tea, etc.

Short Answers

Do	you / they	like cherries?	Yes,	I / we / they	do.	No,	I / we / they	don't.
Does	he / she / it	like cherries?	Yes,	he / she / it	does.	No,	he / she / it	doesn't.

63 Look at the list of activities, then ask each other what you generally do or don't do.

S1: Do you read books? S2: Yes, I do. S2: Do you read newspapers? S3 : No, I don't. etc.

1. read books/newspapers
2. play basketball/tennis
3. do your homework
4. get up early
5. go climbing/swimming
6. tidy your room
7. eat much
8. ride a bicycle
9. go to bed late
10. like sweets
11. watch TV
12. drink milk

64 Look at the pictures then ask and answer as in the example:

Chris's bedroom

Alice's bedroom

1. ...... *Does* ..... he play tennis? .... *Yes, he does.* ....
2. .... she play tennis? ....
3. .... he like coffee? ....
4. .... he like Coke? ....
5. .... they listen to music? ....
6. .... they watch TV? ....
7. .... he tidy his room? ....
8. .... she tidy her room? ....
9. .... she like oranges? ....
10. .... he like cats? ....
11. .... she read books? ....
12. .... she drive a motorcycle? ....

65 Now write what Alice and Chris do or don't do.

.... *Alice plays tennis. Chris doesn't play tennis. He plays football.* ....
.... *Alice doesn't like coffee. She likes Coke.* ....
....
....
....
....
....
....
....
....

66 Fill in the blanks with the correct form of the verbs in brackets.

John Fields 1) .... *is* .... (be) a farmer. He 2) .... (get up) at 5 o'clock in the morning. He 3) .... (wash) and 4) .... (dress). Then he 5) .... (make) breakfast and 6)............... (eat) it. He 7) .... (put on) his coat and 8).............. (go) outside. He 9)............... (milk) the cows early in the morning. His wife, Mary, and the children 10) .... (not/get up) so early. They 11) ....(get up) at 7 o'clock. Mary 12)............ (feed) the chickens and then she 13)............ (make) some tea for herself. The children 14) .... (not/like) tea. They usually 15)............ (drink) milk. At 7.30, Mary 16) .... (take) the children to school. Then she 17) .... (go) to the office and John 18)............ (work) on the farm. At 4 o'clock the children 19) .... (come) home from school. John and Mary 20)............ (cook) dinner. The children 21)............ (not/help) their parents with the cooking but they 22) .... (do) the washing-up. In the evening John and his wife 23) .... (watch) TV or 24) .... (listen) to the radio. The children 25) .... (not/watch) TV. They 26) .... (do) their homework. They all 27) .... (go) to bed at 9 p.m. They 28) .... (be) all very tired.

67 Put the verbs in brackets in the "Present Simple".

My friend Cathy 1) .. *has* .. (have) a horse. It 2) .... (be) a beautiful animal with big eyes and a long tail. Its name is Bella and it 3) .... (love) people. It 4) .... (not / bite) or kick and it is always friendly. It 5) .... (eat) apples and hay but it 6) .... (not / eat) meat. Horses 7) .... (not / like) meat. Cathy usually 8) .... (ride) her horse every day after school. She 9) .... (not / go) into the town because there is too much traffic. There 10) .... (not / be) many cars in the country so she 11) .... (take) Bella there. It often 12) .... (rain) in England so at night Bella and the other horses 13) .... (sleep) in a stable. It 14) .... (not / be) easy looking after a horse but Cathy 15) .... (enjoy) it very much!

68 Fill in the blanks with a verb from the list below in the correct form.

like, live, be, travel, make, say, sing, read, go, write

Michael Johnson 1) .... *lives* ...... in America. He 2) .... a famous pop star. He 3) .... all around the world and 4) .... at pop concerts. He 5) .... his songs too. He also 6) .... pop videos. He 7) .... staying at home and listening to his records. He sometimes 8) .... to expensive restaurants with friends. He also 9) .... a lot of books about strange things. Many people 10) .... he 11) .... a strange man but I 12) .... him very much.

69 a) Say and then write what these people and you like or don't like.

	John		Mary & Chris		Helen		You	

fish	✓			✓	✓			
meat		✓	✓			✓		
carrots	✓			✓		✓		
sweets		✓	✓		✓			

1. John .... *likes fish and carrots but he doesn't like meat or sweets.* ....
2. Mary & Chris ....
3. Helen ....
4. I ....

b) Now ask your partner about his/her likes or dislikes.

e.g. Do you like fish? Yes, I do. etc.

70 Put the adverbs in brackets in the correct place in the sentences.

1. She is late for work. (always) ....*She is always late for work.*......
2. George eats meat. (never) ....
3. You can see foxes in this forest. (sometimes) ....
4. Does Tim go to school by taxi? (usually) ....
5. We spend the summer in France. (usually) ....
6. Tom and James are very busy on Mondays. (often) ....
7. My dog is well-behaved. (rarely) ....
8. Kate doesn't go swimming. (often) ....
9. Simon can do his Maths homework. (never) ....
10. I dance at discos. (seldom) ....

Oral Activity 9

The teacher divides the class into two teams and chooses a leader. Then he / she whispers into the leader's ear "I watch TV". The teams in turn try to guess what the teacher does by asking the leader questions. The teacher invites the students to look at the list of the activities in Exercise 63 for some ideas. The students must guess the answer after only 10 questions. If nobody guesses correctly, the game is a draw. The teacher chooses another leader and you play the game again.

Team A S1 : Does he play tennis?
Leader : No, he doesn't.
Team B S1 : Does he cook dinner?
Leader : No, he doesn't.
Team A S2 : Does he watch TV?
Leader : Yes, he does.

Oral Activity 10

Students in teams say what they don't like. When one student leaves something out his / her team doesn't get a point. Play the game as follows.

Team A S1 : John doesn't like carrots.
Team B S1 : John doesn't like carrots or tomatoes.
Team A S2 : John doesn't like carrots, tomatoes or eggs.
Team B S2 : John doesn't like carrots, eggs or pizza.
Teacher : Wrong! John doesn't like tomatoes either. Team B doesn't get a point.

You can play the game again, this time inviting your students to say what they like.

Writing Activity 3

Write about a typical day in your life.

7. Present Continuous

What's all this noise? What are you doing, Jane?
I'm trying to scare away that mouse. I hate mice.
CRASH
Jane! Why are you standing on the chair and breaking the plates?
CRASH

Affirmative		Negative		Interrogative
Long form	**Short form**	**Long form**	**Short form**	
I **am** talking	I'm talking	I **am not** talking	I'm not talking	**Am** I talking?
You are talking	You're talking	You are not talking	You aren't talking	Are you talking?
He is talking	He's talking	He is not talking	He isn't talking	Is he talking?
She is talking	She's talking	She is not talking	She isn't talking	Is she talking?
It is talking	It's talking	It is not talking	It isn't talking	Is it talking?
We are talking	We're talking	We are not talking	We aren't talking	Are we talking?
You are talking	You're talking	You are not talking	You aren't talking	Are you talking?
They are talking	They're talking	They are not talking	They aren't talking	Are they talking?

We use the Present Continuous for temporary actions or for actions happening at the time of speaking.

Time Expressions used with the Present Continuous		
now	**at the moment**	**at present**

Spelling

When verbs end in one stressed vowel between two consonants, we double the final consonant.	**swim - swimming** **sit - sitting** **stir - stirring**	**BUT**	**walk - walking** **wait - waiting** **open - opening**
Look at the spelling of these verbs :	**lie - lying** **die - dying etc**		**write - writing** **drive - driving etc**

71 Add "-ing" to the following verbs and put them in the correct list.

make, begin, hit, sit, shave, drink, play, lie, fly, die, cut, sleep, smoke, meet, take, type, drop

+ ing	~~-ie~~ ➡ y + ing	~~-e~~ ➡ ing	double consonant + ing
1. .... *drinking*	1.	1.	1. ....
2.	2.	2.	2. ....
3.	3.	3.	3. ....
4.	4.	4.	4. ....
5.	5.	5.	5. ....

72 Fill in as in the example :

Long form	Short form
1. He ..... *is* ....feeding the dog.	He..*'s*............................. feeding the dog.
2. They .... reading.	They .... reading.
3. It ....flying.	It .... flying.
4. We .... not cleaning the floor.	We .... cleaning the floor.
5. He .... not crying.	He .... crying.
6. You .... listening.	You .... listening.

73 Look at the picture and the list of verbs, then complete the text.

do, open, look, snow, stay, read, sit, listen, sleep, sing

It is Christmas Day. Mrs Huston 1) *is reading a* newspaper. Mr Huston 2) .... the washing-up. The boys 3) .... Christmas carols. Grandfather and Grandmother 4) .... on the sofa. Grandmother 5) .... to the boys singing but Grandfather 6) .... The girls 7) .... their presents. The dog 8) .... at the girls. It is very cold. It 9) .... outside and so the Hustons 10) .... at home tonight.

Short answers

Are	you / they	listening?	Yes,	we / they	are.	No,	we / they	aren't.
Is	he / she / it	listening?	Yes,	he / she / it	is.	No,	he / she / it	isn't.

74 Ask and answer as in the examples :

1. (laugh?)
   ..Is she laughing?.
   .. No, she isn't. ....
   .. She's crying. ....

2. (eat?)
   Is the dog eating?
   .. Yes, it is. ......
   .... It's eating. ..

3. (write?)
   ....
   ....
   ....

4. (play the piano?)
   ....
   ....
   ....

5. (ski?)
   ....
   ....
   ....

6. (dance?)
   ....
   ....
   ....

7. (jump?)
   ....
   ....
   ....

8. (watch TV?)
   ....
   ....
   ....

75 Put the verbs in brackets into the "Present Continuous".

This is London airport. Many people 1) .. are waiting . (wait) to go on holiday. The woman at the check-in desk 2) .... (take) the passengers' tickets and she 3) ....(ask) them some questions. At "Passport Control" a man who 4) .... (wear) a uniform 5) .... (look) at everyone's passports. Some people 6) .... (sit) on chairs and while they 7) .... (wait) they 8) .... (read) books or magazines. There is a bar where a man 9) .... (serve) tea and coffee. Outside, a plane 10) .... (take off) and another one 11) .... (come down). Some men 12) .... (put) the passengers' bags onto another plane. A man who 13) .... (leave) 14) .... (say) goodbye to his family.

Writing Activity 4

First say then write, what you, your teacher and classmates are doing and wearing now.
e.g. I'm wearing a blue dress and black shoes. I'm sitting and writing. John is ... etc.

76 Look at the picture and write sentences as in the example :

1. The man on the rock is sleeping. .. *No! The man on the rock isn't sleeping. He's fishing.* .....
2. The two boys are lying on the sand. ....
3. The woman is crying. ....
4. The fat boy is laughing. ....
5. The dog is eating. ....
6. The man and woman are playing with the ball. ....
7. The two girls are water-skiing. ....
8. The young man is reading. ....

Oral Activity 11

The teacher divides the class into two teams. Both teams look at the picture in Exercise 76. One team asks questions and the other answers the questions with books open. Each correct question or answer gets 1 point. The winning team is the one which gets the most points.

Team A S1 : Is the man on the rock swimming?
Team B S1 : No, he isn't swimming. He's fishing.

Team A S2 : Is the woman playing?
Team B S2 : Yes, she's playing.
Teacher : Wrong! The woman isn't playing. She's lying on the sand. (2 points for team A, 1 point for team B)

Play the game again with Team B asking questions and Team A answering them.

Writing Activity 5

Find a picture from a magazine and write what the people in it are wearing and doing.

Present Simple versus Present Continuous

We use Present Simple for permanent states, repeated or habitual actions.	We use Present Continuous for temporary states or actions or for actions happening at the moment of speaking.
Time expressions used with Present S.	**Time expressions used with Pres. Cont.**
every day / week / month / year, usually, often, always, rarely, never, sometimes, in the morning / evening / afternoon, at night etc.	now, at present, at the moment, today, tonight

My wife usually reads the newspaper and I watch TV in the evening.

Today, it's my wife's birthday and we're going out for dinner.

Some verbs are usually used only in the Simple tenses.

believe, belong, decide, forget, hate, hear, know, like, love, need, remember, smell, see, think, understand, want etc.

The verb "have" is used only in the Simple tenses when it means "possess". Otherwise, it is used in the Continuous tenses as well.

I **have** two cars at present. **BUT** She **is having** a bath now.

77 State which situations are permanent and which are temporary, then write sentences as in the example:

Usually

.. *permanent* ....

1. pilot / fly / a plane

.. *He is a pilot. He* .. *usually flies a plane.*

Today

.. *temporary* ....

2. ride / a horse

. *Today he is riding* . .. *a horse.* ....

3. cooks / cook

....

....

....

4. eat / in a restaurant

....

....

....

78 Put the verbs in brackets into the "Present Simple" or "Present Continuous".

Today 1) .*is*.. (be) very cold and it 2) .... (snow). It always 3) .... (snow) here in December. Peter 4) .... (swim) in the sea now. He 5) .... (like) fish and he 6) .... (love) cold weather. Peter's friend 7) .... (watch) him. Peter always 8) .... (bring) his friend a fish. His friend 9) .... (wait) for his fish. Peter 10) .... (not/cook) his fish, he 11) .... (eat) it in the sea. This 12) .... (not/be) strange because Peter is a penguin!

79 Choose a time expression from the box to complete the sentences.

every day, in the evening, now, often, at the moment, rarely,
in the morning, today, at present, on Saturdays, usually, never

1. Mother does her shopping ...... *on Saturdays* ....
2. We go to school ....
3. He can't talk to you. He is talking on the phone ....
4. They .... go to work on Sundays. They stay at home.
5. We can't go out. It is raining ....
6. She .... walks her dog but .... her mother is walking the dog.
7. We eat breakfast ....
8. She's eating lunch ....
9. Father and Mother watch TV ....
10. He .... eats sweets. He doesn't like them very much.
11. He likes sports. He .... plays tennis.

80 Put the verbs in brackets into the "Present Simple" or "Present Continuous".

1. He often ..... *goes* .... (go) to the cinema.
2. They .... (watch) TV at the moment.
3. John is outside. He .... (wash) the car.
4. Nina usually .... (drive) to work.
5. Father .... (lie) on the sofa now.
6. Claire .... (not / like) pizza.

81 Put the verbs in brackets into the "Present Simple" or "Present Continuous".

Dear Susan,
*Here I 1) ... **am** ... (be) in sunny Greece. The weather 2) .... (be) fantastic. We 3) .... (have) a wonderful time. At the moment I 4) .... (lie) beside the swimming pool with my friend James. I 5) .... (sunbathe) and James 6) .... (drink) lemonade. We 7) .... (sunbathe) and we 8) .... (swim) every day and at night we 9) .... (eat) in a restaurant and then we 10) .... (dance) in the disco. I 11) .... (have) a good sun-tan. I 12) .... (look forward) to seeing you next week when we 13) .... (come) home.*

See you then.
Love, Sally

Miss S. Jones,
38 Dean Park, Peebles
Border Region

82 Choose the correct item.

1. Look at him! He .... *C* .... a boat.
   A) rows B) rowing C) is rowing
2. He usually .... tennis in the afternoon.
   A) plays B) play C) is playing
3. What .... in the kitchen, Peter?
   A) do you B) are you doing C) you do
4. She .... dinner now.
   A) is having B) have C) has
5. He .... a comic every day.
   A) read B) is reading C) reads
6. Be quiet! The baby ....
   A) sleep B) sleeps C) is sleeping
7. I .... a letter now.
   A) write B) am writing C) writes
8. Look! The dog .... with the ball.
   A) play B) is playing C) are playing

83 Complete the blanks with a verb from the box in the correct tense.

travel, work, read, sell, rain, go, look, carry, laugh, wear

Mr Simmons 1) .... *is travelling* ..... by train. He 2) .... to work. He 3) .... in a shop. He 4) .... video games. He 5) .... the newspaper at the moment and he 6) .... because he 7) .... at a funny cartoon. He 8) .... a hat and he 9) .... an umbrella with him because it 10) .... today.

84 Find the mistakes, then underline and correct them.

Today is Saturday and we <u>is</u> at the shopping centre. Every Saturday my mother is taking me shopping with her. She is wanting to buy a new skirt but she not like the one that the lady showing her. I am hating shopping with my mother. She never know what to buy. I look at some lovely trousers now and I want to buy them but I am not having enough money.

1. ... *are* ..... 2. .... 3. .... 4. .... 5. ....
6. .... 7. .... 8. .... 9. ....

Oral Activity 12

Look again at Exercise 73 p 41. See Oral Activity 11 p 43 for instructions.

Writing Activity 6

Imagine that it is 9 p.m. and you are at home. Write what your father, mother, brother, grandmother etc are doing at the moment and what they usually do at this time every day.

Example : Father is reading his newspaper. He usually reads it in the evening. etc.

8. Past Simple

Jean, you look terrible! What happened to you? Did you enjoy the party?
Well, not really. Tom drank too much. He fell off his chair and pushed me into the swimming pool. I got wet so I didn't stay at the party.

Regular verbs:

We form the Past Simple of regular verbs by adding -ed.

Affirmative	Negative		Interrogative
	Long form	**Short form**	
I stayed	I did not stay	I didn't stay	Did I stay?
You stayed	You did not stay	You didn't stay	Did you stay?
He stayed	He did not stay	He didn't stay	Did he stay?
She stayed	She did not stay	She didn't stay	Did she stay?
It stayed	It did not stay	It didn't stay	Did it stay?
We stayed	We did not stay	We didn't stay	Did we stay?
You stayed	You did not stay	You didn't stay	Did you stay?
They stayed	They did not stay	They didn't stay	Did they stay?

Spelling

-e ➡ -d	double consonant + ed	consonant + y ➡ -ied	vowel + y ➡ -yed
like - liked	**prefer - preferred**	**carry - carried**	**play - played**
hate - hated	**stop - stopped**	**study - studied**	**enjoy - enjoyed**
close - closed	**travel - travelled**	**tidy - tidied**	**stay - stayed**

85 Write the "Past Simple" of the following verbs.

1. open .. *opened*....
2. love ....
3. plan ....
4. empty ....
5. regret ....
6. quarrel ....
7. try ....
8. die ....
9. cry ....
10. fry ....
11. smoke ....
12. play ....

Pronunciation

86 Add -ed to the verbs, put them in the correct column and read them out.

arrive, close, help, want, hurry, look, watch, clean, cook, regret, rob, visit, add, push, start, live, end, wait, count, like, travel, tidy, laugh, finish, kiss, post, change, open

/ɪd/		/t/		/d/	
after /t/, /d/		after /k/, /s/, /tʃ/, /ʃ/, /f/ , /p/		after other sounds	
counted	....	kissed	....	opened	....
....	....	....	....	....	....
....	....	....	....	....	....
....	....	....	....	....	....
....	....	....	....	....	....
....	....	....	....	....	....

Irregular verbs have a special past form.

Present	I go	I drink	I am
Past	I went	I drank	I was

See List of Irregular Verbs at the end of the book.

Past Simple of the verb "to be"

Affirmative	I was, You were, He/She/It was, We were, You were, They were
Interrogative	Was I?, Were you?, Was he/she it?, Were we?, Were you?, Were they?
Negative	I was not, You were not, He/She/It was not, We were not, You were not, They were not
short form	I wasn't, You weren't, He/She/It wasn't, We weren't, You weren't, They weren't

87 Fill in the blanks with "am", "is", "are", "was" or "were".

Today I 1) .. am .. at home. It 2) .... Saturday morning and it 3) .... very cold. It's only a month since my family and I 4) .... on holiday in Portugal. The weather 5) .... fantastic; it 6) .... really hot and sunny. We 7) .... all happy then. It 8) .... not long ago, of course, but I 9) .... already missing the sun and the sea. Well, it 10) .... nice to be back home with all our friends.

88 Look at the List of Irregular Verbs at the end of the book and fill in the blanks.

Present	Past	Present	Past
go	... *went*	finish	....
have/has	....	meet	....
....	came	....	sang
is / are	....	speak	....

We use the Past Simple for actions which finished at a stated time in the past . The Past Simple is used with time expressions of the past.

Time expressions used with the Past Simple			
yesterday then	last night / week / month / year a week / month / year ago	two days ago in 1980	when etc.

89 Choose a verb from the box to fill in the blanks with "Present" or "Past Simple".

finish, go, have, be

Usually

Yesterday

James usually 1) ... *finishes* ... work at 4.30 p.m. Yesterday he 2) .... work at 1.00 p.m. He usually 3) .... home by train. Yesterday he 4) .... home by taxi. He usually 5) .... dinner at home. Yesterday he 6) .... dinner in a restaurant with his friends. He usually 7) .... to bed early. Yesterday he 8) .... to bed late because it 9) .... his birthday.

90 Look at the List of Irregular Verbs at the end of the book and fill in the blanks.

Present	Past	Present	Past
... *have*	had	begin	....
....	cut	do	....
take	....	leave	....
steal	....	shine	....
drink	....	....	became
....	put	hear	....
make	....	write	....
can	....	say	....
find	....	get	....
run	....	see	....
tell	....	hold	....

91 Fill in the blanks with the "Past Simple" of the correct verbs from the list.

put up, cook, go, make, take, collect, drink, meet, speak, play, feel, sing

Last weekend I 1) .... *went* ...... camping with my friends. We 2) .... tents and sleeping bags. Three of us 3) .... the tents while the others 4) .... wood and 5) .... a fire. We 6) .... potatoes and 7) .... Coke. In the evening, Tom 8) .... the guitar and everybody 9) .... songs. We 10) .... some French tourists and 11) ....to them in French. At about midnight, we all 12) .... sleepy, so we 13) .... to bed.

92 Fill in the blanks with a time expression from the list below:

at the moment, always, two months ago, in 1986, last night, every weekend, last summer

1. We saw a really good film at the cinema .... *last night* ....
2. They went to Egypt for the whole month of August ....
3. My parents do the shopping ....
4. He finished school ....
5. I am working .... I can't come with you.
6. She .... sneezes when she is near a cat; she's allergic to them.
7. He passed his driving test ....

93 Put the verbs in brackets into the correct tense.

1. He often ...... *brings* ...... (bring) me flowers.
2. .... (you / meet) Paul yesterday?
3. Father .... (work) in the garden now.
4. What .... (you / do) at the moment?
5. Mr Jones .... (paint) his house last month.
6. She .... (go) to school on foot every day.
7. It .... (be) hot yesterday.
8. The baby .... (not / sleep) now.
9. He never .... (drive) fast.
10. She .... (leave) Paris in 1987.

Short answers						
	Yes,	I/you/he/she/it	did.	No,	I/you/he/she/it	didn't.
		we/you/they			we/you/they	

94 Ask and answer as in the example :

	go for a walk	play golf	write a letter	wash the car
Peter	✓	✓		
Sally		✓	✓	
Mr & Mrs Page	✓			✓
You				

1. Peter / play golf? ...... *Did Peter play golf yesterday? Yes, he did.* ......
2. Peter / wash the car? ....
3. Peter / write a letter? ....
4. Sally / go for a walk? ....
5. Sally / play golf? ....
6. Sally / wash the car? ....
7. Mr & Mrs Page / play golf? ....
8. Mr & Mrs Page / write a letter? ....

Now write short paragraphs as in the example :

1. Peter .... *went for a walk and played golf. He didn't write a letter or wash the car.* ......
2. Sally ....
....
3. Mr and Mrs Page ....
....
4. I ....
....

95 Put the verbs in brackets into the "Past Simple".

Pamela : What 1) .... did you do ..... (you / do) last weekend?
Tony : I 2) .... (go) to my cousin's house.
Pamela : 3) .... (be) it far?
Tony : No, it only 4) .... (take) us 30 minutes.
Pamela : 5) .... (you / stay) there long?
Tony : We 6) .... (stay) only for the weekend.
What 7) .... (you / do) last weekend?
Pamela : My family and I 8) .... (take) the dog and we
9) .... (have) a picnic on the beach.
Tony : 10) .... (be) it sunny?
Pamela : Yes, the sun 11) .... (shine) all day.

96 Put the verbs in brackets into the "Past Simple".

Bryan Adams comes from Canada. He 1) .... left .... (leave) school at sixteen and 2) .... (work) as a gardener. He 3) .... (start) his career as a singer at the age of eighteen. He 4) .... (work) hard then. He only 5) .... (become) famous in 1987 when he 6) .... (make) his first album which he 7) .... (call) "Reckless". After "Reckless" no one 8) .... (hear) about him for a while, until 1991 when he 9) .... (sing) "Everything I Do, I Do It for You" which 10) .... (be) a great success. After that he 11) .... (go) on a world tour. Today, Bryan Adams is back in Canada enjoying his success.

97 Put the verbs in brackets into the "Present Simple" or "Past Simple".

Tommy Brown 1) .... is .... (be) a real story-teller. No one 2) .... (believe) what he 3) .... (say) because he always 4) .... (tell) lies. He 5) .... (live) in a small village and 6) .... (work) on a farm near his village.

One night last week Tommy 7) .... (finish) work late. It 8) .... (be) dark and cold. Suddenly he 9) .... (hear) a strange noise so he 10) .... (look) up. It 11) .... (be) a UFO with bright flashing lights. It 12) .... (come down) towards him and he 13) .... (see) two green men looking at him. He 14) .... (scream), 15) .... (drop) his bag and 16) .... (run away).

When he 17) .... (arrive) at the village he 18) .... (meet) some villagers and 19) .... (start) to tell them the news but they all 20) .... (laugh) at him. No one 21) .... (believe) Tommy.

98 Choose a verb from the list and complete the text using the "Past Simple".

decide, get into, drive, find, take, start, tell, pack, move, begin, see, run away, can, be, have, get out, mend,arrive, go

Last Sunday the Smiths 1) ... *decided* ... to go on a picnic, so they all 2) .... the car and 3) .... to the country. They 4) .... a nice place in a field and 5) .... the food out of the basket. As soon as they 6) .... to eat an angry farmer 7) .... them to get off his land. They 8) .... everything up again and 9) .... to another field. The moment they 10) .... to eat, they 11) .... a bull running towards them. They 12) .... as fast as they 13) .... It 14) .... raining very hard so they 15) .... the car to go home. They 16) .... not even half-way home when they 17) .... a puncture. They 18) .... of the car and 19) .... it. When they 20) .... home, they 21) .... wet and miserable. They 22) .... a cup of tea and 23) .... to bed.

Oral Activity 13

Cover the text of Exercise 98. Look at the pictures and the list of verbs and try to retell the story .

99 Write what they and you had or didn't have at the age of six.

	doll	walkman	teddy bear	school bag
Phil		✓	✓	✓
Cherry	✓		✓	✓
You				

1. Phil ...... *didn't have a doll but he had a walkman, a teddy bear and a* .... *school bag when he was six.* ....

2. Cherry ....
....

3. I ....
....

Oral Activity 14 (Question and answer game)

Both teams look at the text for Exercise 96. See Oral Activity 11 for instructions.

Oral Activity 15 (Chain story)

"An Exciting Weekend". The teacher divides the class into two teams, then writes the word list on the board and explains the new words to the students. He / she starts the story and invites the teams in turn to continue it. Each correct sentence gets 1 point. The team which fails to continue the story doesn't get a point.

Word list: **go shopping, see somebody stealing, shout loudly, catch the thief, leave bag on bus, run down the road, give back the bag, hear someone screaming, neighbour's house on fire, telephone fire-station, put the fire out**

Writing Activity 7

Write a letter to a friend about how you spent your weekend. (80 - 100 words).

Revision Exercises II

100 Choose the correct item.

1. It .... *C* .... now.
   A) snows B) snowed C) is snowing
2. Have we got .... milk?
   A) some B) any C) many
3. There isn't .... in the kitchen.
   A) anybody B) somebody C) nobody
4. Do you like spaghetti? Yes, ...
   A) do I B) I do C) I don't
5. I've got .... money. I can buy an ice-cream.
   A) a little B) a few C) little
6. There are so .... plants in the garden!
   A) much B) little C) many
7. She .... tennis well.
   A) play B) doesn't play C) don't play
8. Ann .... coffee now!
   A) drank B) drink C) is drinking
9. Look at him! He ....
   A) is swimming B) swam C) swims
10. There's .... bread in the cupboard.
    A) little B) few C) many
11. She .... to school yesterday.
    A) is going B) goes C) went
12. This book .... to me.
    A) belongs B) belong C) is belonging
13. We .... abroad last summer.
    A) travel B) travels C) travelled
14. .... name is Jim Smith.
    A) He B) His C) Him
15. She's got .... cheese.
    A) some B) a C) an
16. These are the .... dresses.
    A) girls's B) girl C) girls'

101 Find the mistake and correct it.

1. There isn't ~~something~~ good on TV. .... *anything* ......
2. She's got two puppys. ....
3. She writes a letter last Monday. ....
4. There isn't some fruit in the fridge. ....
5. She have got a big nose. ....
6. He is knowing my father. ....
7. Moira didn't came to school yesterday. ....
8. He lives anywhere near the new cinema. ....
9. Paula always sing in the bath. ....
10. She has a bath at the moment. ....
11. Look at they car! ....
12. They are goods teachers. ....
13. We've got very few cheese. ....
14. I doesn't know his name. ....

102 Put the verbs in brackets into the "Present Simple" or "Present Continuous".

Helen: Hello. I 1) ... *want* ... (want) to speak to Bob, please. 2) .... (he/be) there?
Man: No, he 3) .... (not/be). He 4) .... (work) at his office at the moment. He always 5) .... (work) there in the afternoons.
Helen: Well, can I speak to his mother or father, please?
Man: Sorry, but they 6) .... (stay) with some friends in the country this weekend. They 7) .... (visit) them once a month.
Helen: What about Jane? What 8) .... (she/do)?
Man: She 9) .... (swim) in the pool with her friends now.
Helen: Well, it 10) .... (seem) this 11) .... (not/be) my lucky day. Can you tell Bob to call me when he 12) .... (come) back home?

103 Put the verbs in brackets into the "Present Simple" or "Past Simple".

This 1) ... *is* ... (be) my dog, Blackie. He 2) .... (be) a small black dog with a bushy tail. Every day I 3) .... (take) him for a walk to the park. He 4) .... (run) everywhere and 5) .... (play) with his ball on the grass. When we 6) .... (come) back he 7) .... (eat) his food and then he 8) .... (lie) on the carpet. At night he 9) .... (sleep) on a rug near my bed. One day last year I 10) .... (take) him for a walk but I 11) .... (lose) him. He 12) .... (not/be) anywhere. I 13) .... (go) home and 14) .... (tell) my parents. They 15) .... (search) the park and then they 16) ....(go) to the police. A few days later a policeman 17) .... (come) to my house. Blackie 18) .... (be) with him. I 19) .... (be) very happy to see him back home.

104 Fill in "few", "a few", "little" or "a little".

Sally's mother is standing at the kitchen table. In front of her there is 1) .... *a little* .... milk, 2) .... butter, 3) .... nuts, 4) .... raisins and 5) .... flour. She wants to make a cake but she has got 6) .... sugar and 7) .... eggs so she can't make one. She is waiting for Sally to bring her the sugar and the eggs she needs.

105 Fill in "it", "their", "his", "her" or "he".

Kate and 1) ... *her* .... brother are walking 2) .... dog, Rufus. Rufus wants to chase 3) .... ball, but Kate's brother is keeping it in 4) .... pocket because 5) .... is afraid the dog will lose 6) ....

106 Fill in the blanks using "some", "any" or "no".

Sally: I'm going to the supermarket to buy 1) .. *some* .. things. There's 2) .... milk in the fridge and we haven't got 3) .... coffee. Do you need anything?
Julie: Can you buy 4) .... biscuits, please?
Sally: Yes, of course. Anything else?
Julie: Oh, and 5) .... flour because I want to make 6) .... cakes this afternoon.
Sally: But you made cakes yesterday. Aren't there 7) .... left?
Julie: No. My friends came last night and they ate them all!

107 Look at the table, first say and then write about Ann and yourself.

	be happy		go shopping		have parties		get up early		help Mother		drink wine	
	Ann	You	Ann	You	Ann	You	Ann	You	Ann	You	Ann	You
often					✓							
never							✓					
usually									✓			
always	✓											
rarely											✓	
sometimes			✓									

Ann ... *is always happy. She* ....
....
....
I ....
....
....

108 Fill in "some", "any", "no" or their derivatives.

Chris was on his way home last night when 1) .... *something* .... happened to his car and it stopped. He looked at the engine but he couldn't see 2) .... wrong. He tried to start the car again but 3) .... happened. Then he realised that there was 4) .... petrol left. Chris didn't know what to do. There was 5) .... else on the road and Chris couldn't think of 6) .... to find 7) .... petrol so late at night. Suddenly 8) .... came past on a bicycle. Luckily, he lived nearby and ten minutes later he returned with 9) .... petrol. Chris didn't have 10) .... money to pay for it, so he took the man's address and said he would send him 11) .... money later.

9. Present Perfect

Have / has + past participle

I've just tidied the house and fixed the TV.
What have you done George?
WET PAINT
I've just painted the bench you're sitting on.

Regular Verbs

Affirmative		Negative		Interrogative
Long form	**Short form**	**Long form**	**Short form**	
I have walked	I've walked	I have not walked	I haven't walked	Have I walked?
You have walked	You've walked	You have not walked	You haven't walked	Have you walked?
He has walked	He's walked	He has not walked	He hasn't walked	Has he walked?
She has walked	She's walked	She has not walked	She hasn't walked	Has she walked?
It has walked	It's walked	It has not walked	It hasn't walked	Has it walked?
We have walked	We've walked	We have not walked	We haven't walked	Have we walked?
You have walked	You've walked	You have not walked	You haven't walked	Have you walked?
They have walked	They've walked	They have not walked	They haven't walked	Have they walked?

Spelling

stop - stopped	**study - studied**	**type - typed**
prefer - preferred	**play - played**	**smoke - smoked**

Irregular Verbs

Affirmative		Negative		Interrogative
Long form	**Short form**	**Long form**	**Short form**	
I have eaten	I've eaten	I have not eaten	I haven't eaten	Have I eaten?
You have eaten	You've eaten	You have not eaten	You haven't eaten	Have you eaten?
He has eaten	He's eaten	He has not eaten	He hasn't eaten	Has he eaten?
She has eaten	She's eaten	She has not eaten	She hasn't eaten	Has she eaten?
It has eaten	It's eaten	It has not eaten	It hasn't eaten	Has it eaten?
We have eaten	We've eaten	We have not eaten	We haven't eaten	Have we eaten?
You have eaten	You've eaten	You have not eaten	You haven't eaten	Have you eaten?
They have eaten	They've eaten	They have not eaten	They haven't eaten	Have they eaten?

Look at the end of the book for the past participles of irregular verbs.

Present Perfect versus Past Simple

Time expressions used with Pres. Perf.	Time expressions used with Past Simple
just, ever, never, already, yet, always, how long, so far, for, since, recently	**yesterday, last night / week / month / year, ago, then, when, in 1972 etc.**
1. We use Present Perfect for recent actions or states or for actions which happened at an unstated time in the past.	**1. We use Past Simple for actions or states which finished at a stated time in the past.**

I **have bought** a new car. (**When** did he buy it? **We don't know**.) (unstated time)	I **bought** this car ten years ago. (**When** did he buy it? Ten years **ago**.) (stated time)
2. We use Present Perfect for actions or states which began in the past and continue up to the present.	**2. We use Past Simple for actions or states which finished in the past.**

I **have been** a clerk for two years. (He is still a clerk.)	I **was** a clerk for seven years. (He isn't a clerk now, he is a businessman.)

"Since" is used to express a starting point in the past.	"For" is used for a period of time.
She's been ill **since** Monday.	She's been ill **for** two days.

109 Write the past participles of the following verbs.

1. eat ... *eaten* ....
2. sleep ....
3. open ....
4. find ....
5. give ....
6. iron ....
7. clean ....
8. take ....
9. swim ....
10. write ....
11. arrive ....
12. put ....
13. leave ....
14. drink ....
15. talk ....
16. break ....
17. make ....
18. run ....
19. buy ....
20. have ....

110 Complete the sentences as in the example :

Long form	Short form
1. She ..... *has* ....cleaned the house.	She..*'s* .... cleaned the house.
2. We .... not worked hard.	We .... worked hard.
3. I .... visited them several times.	I .... visited them several times.
4. She .... not finished yet.	She .... finished yet.
5. They .... talked to him.	They .... talked to him.

111 Choose a verb from the list, use the "Present Perfect" and complete the sentences.

drink - break - leave - make - start - phone - clean - arrive - wash

1. She .. *has just broken*.... .... a vase.

2. We .... the room.

3. I .... the beds.

4. He .... his friend.

5. The plane ....

6. It .... raining.

7. The bus ....

8. They .... their hair.

9. You .... a glass of beer.

112 Fill in "since" or "for".

1. ..... *since*.............. 1945
2. .... yesterday
3. .... six days
4. .... a month
5. .... two weeks
6. .... last month

Short answers

Have you / they come?	Yes, I / we / they have.	No, I / we / they haven't.
Has he / she / it come?	Yes, he / she / it has.	No, he / she / it hasn't.

113 Ask and answer as in the example :

	visit / Brazil	play / the guitar	climb / a mountain	see / a crocodile	ride / a camel
Mary		✓		✓	✓
Tony	✓		✓	✓	
You					

1. ..... *Has Mary ever visited Brazil? No, she hasn't. Has Mary ever played the guitar?* ...
..... *Yes, she has.* ....
....
....

2. ....
....
....
....
....

3. Have you ....
....
....
....
....

114 Put the verbs into the "Present Perfect" or "Past Simple".

a) Ann : 1) ..... *Did you go* .... (you / go) on holiday last year?
Paul : Yes, I 2) .... (go) to Spain. 3) .... (you / ever / be) there?
Ann : Yes, I 4) .... (go) there last year too.

b) Maria : I 5) .... (sell) my old radio.
Helen : Really? When 6) .... (you / sell) it?
Maria : I 7) .... (sell) it yesterday.

c) Ian : I 8) .... (go) to the new sports centre yesterday.
John : Really? I 9) .... (not / be) there yet. What's it like?
Ian : It's fabulous! I 10) .... (never / see) such a fantastic sports centre before.

115 Fill in with "yet", "ago", "ever", "last night", "for" or "since".

1. My father went to Spain two days .... *ago* ....
2. He has known her .... 1990.
3. She hasn't finished her work ....
4. Have you .... seen an elephant?
5. We went to bed at 10 o'clock ....
6. He has been in Madrid .... ten years.

116 Put the verbs into the "Past Simple" or "Present Perfect".

1. I .... *haven't finished* .... (not/finish) my homework yet.
2. We .... (not/see) him since he .... (leave) school.
3. We .... (go) to bed very early last night because we .... (be) tired.
4. They .... (move) to London two years ago.
5. She .... (not/ring) me since Tuesday.
6. I .... (just/see) a very interesting programme on TV.
7. Laura .... (never/be) to France.
8. I .... (see) an old friend of mine last week.
9. I .... (not/be) to a disco for months.
10. My little sister .... (not/learn) to read yet.

117 Peter has many jobs to do at home this weekend. Write what he has "already" done or not "yet" done.

1. tidy the bedroom	✓	6. take the dog for a walk	✗
2. clean the floor	✗	7. iron his clothes	✓
3. wash the dishes	✗	8. wash his car	✓
4. water the plants	✗	9. tidy the kitchen	✗
5. do the shopping	✓	10. mend the kettle	✗

1. .... *He has already tidied the bedroom.* ....
2. .... *He hasn't cleaned the floor yet.* ....
3. ....
4. ....
5. ....
6. ....
7. ....
8. ....
9. ....
10. ....

118 Put the verbs into the "Present Simple", "Present Perfect" or "Past Simple".

Nigel Hurricane 1) .... *drives* .... (drive) racing cars. This year he 2) .... (come) first in eight races so far and 3) .... (win) the World Championship. He 4) .... (learn) to drive in 1969 and 5) .... (start) to race fast cars ten years later. He 6) .... (earn) a lot of money and he 7) .... (become) very famous. He now 8) .... (live) in America. He 9) .... (get) married three years ago and he 10) .... (have) two children.

119 Tick the correct box as in the example:

	since	for	
I haven't seen him	✓		last summer.
			1985.
			a long time.
			last month.
			two weeks.

120 Fill in the blanks with "for" or "since".

1. Ben : How long have you known John?
   Alex : I've known him ... *since* ..... we were at school.
2. Sue : How long have you worn contact lenses?
   Emma : I've worn them .... five years.
3. Jim : How long have you and Bob lived in France?
   Tina : We've lived here .... over ten years now.
4. Andy : I'm sorry I'm late. How long have you been here?
   Tom : I've been here .... 5 o'clock.
5. Sarah : How long have you had that dress?
   Angie : I've had it .... Christmas.
6. Joe : How long have you been in Asia?
   Mary : I've been in Asia .... seven years.
7. Cherry : How long have you worked at this school?
   Terry : I've worked at this school .... 1963.
8. Helen : How long have you known Tom?
   Nick : I've known him .... five years.
9. George : When did you last go to America?
   Anna : I haven't been to America .... July, 1979.

121 Put the verbs in brackets into the "Past Simple" or "Present Perfect".

I love winter sports. 1) I *'ve been* ..(be) ice-skating many times. When I was younger I 2) .... (go) to an ice-rink with my school. I 3) .... (fall) over a lot and I 4) .... (can/not) skate very well, but I really 5) .... (enjoy) it. Then last year I 6) .... (visit) Austria and 7) .... (skate) at an outdoor rink there. I 8) .... (also/play) ice hockey. I 9) .... (never/ski) though. I 10) .... (go) on holiday to Switzerland last month to go skiing, but on the first day I 11) .... (slip) on some ice and 12) .... (break) my ankle, so I 13) .... (can/not) ski at all.

122 Put the verbs in brackets into the "Present Perfect" or "Past Simple".

1. Kevin ...... *has lost* ...... (lose) his key. He .... (leave) it on the bus yesterday.
2. I .... (not / play) tennis since I was at school but I .... (be) very good at it then.
3. Mr and Mrs Little .... (visit) Egypt. They .... (go) there on their honeymoon in 1967.
4. A: .... you .... (not / choose) a dress for the party next week yet?
   B: Yes, I .... (buy) one yesterday.
5. A: .... you .... (not / sell) your old car yet?
   B: Yes, my cousin .... (give) me £500 for it last week.
6. I think our teacher .... (forget) about the test! He .... (not / say) anything about it in the last lesson!
7. Sarah .... (break) her leg. She .... (fall) off a horse last week.
8. We .... (sell) our house. Some people .... (see) it last month and .... (buy) it.
9. I .... (finish) decorating my room. I .... (paint) it last week and I .... (put up) the new curtains last night.
10. They .... (lose) their cat. It .... (run) away last week.
11. Peter .... (pass) his driving test. He .... (take) it last Friday.
12. We .... (know) Kate since last year. We .... (meet) her at a party.
13. I .... (never / be) to Australia. I .... (want) to go last summer but I .... (can / not).
14. I .... (not / be) out since we .... (move) to our new house.
15. Tom .... (see) this film twice. The last time he .... (see) it .... (be) a week ago.

123 Put the verbs in brackets into the "Past Simple" or the "Present Perfect".

MAN FINDS TWO-TAILED MONKEY

Scientists 1) .... *have discovered* .... (discover) a new animal in the jungle recently. They believe it 2) .... (exist) for a million years. The animal 3) .... (develop) two tails for moving between the trees and eyes that can see in the dark. John Jones 4) .... (find) the animal when he 5) .... (explore) the northern Ablu jungle. He 6) .... (see) the animal on a tree so he 7) .... (stop) and 8) .... (catch) it. "I 9) .... (always / want) to discover something new but I 10) .... (not/think) it would be an animal as I 11) .... (study) plants for twenty years," he 12) .... (say) yesterday. The Bronx Zoo 13) .... (buy) the animal. They 14) .... (show) it to the public yesterday.

124 Joe's Aunt is writing to him with her latest news. Fill in the gaps using either the "Past Simple" or the "Present Perfect" form of the verbs in brackets.

Dear Joe,

Everything is fine at home. John 1) .. **has finished** .. (finish) writing a book and Paula 2) .... (take) her exams. Yesterday, I 3) .... (see) a film at the local cinema. It 4) .... (be) very good. After that I 5) .... (drive) to London and 6) .... (meet) your father. He 7) .... (go) to London last Friday to give a lecture. Your father looks different. He 8) .... (grow) a moustache and 9) .... (lose) a lot of weight. I have to go now. Your father 10) .... (just / wake up) and I have to take him to the station. Hope to hear from you soon.

Love,
Aunt Emma

125 **Mrs Dune is a terrible gossip. She is telling her neighbour the latest news of the neighbourhood.**

Danny and Susan 1) ... *have just returned* ..... (just/return) from their holiday. They 2) .... (be) in New York for a week. The Browns 3) .... (move) into their new house. They 4) .... (sell) the old one two weeks ago. Sandra 5) .... (buy) an expensive computer. She 6) .... (buy) it yesterday. John 7) .... (take) his car to the garage. He 8) .... (take) it there at 9 o'clock on Friday. Mrs Gate 9) .... (not/tidy) her house yet. She 10) .... (go) for a walk. She 11) .... (leave) about two hours ago and 12) .... (not/come) back yet. Mr Moore 13) .... (already/cut) the grass but he 14) .... (not/paint) the fence yet.

Oral Activity 16

The teacher divides the class into two teams and writes a list of time words/expressions on the board. The teams in turn make sentences using "for" or "since" and an appropriate verb in the Present Perfect. Each correct answer gets 1 point. The team with the most points is the winner.

List : two hours, last week, Christmas, last summer, a long time, Tuesday, a week, three days, 1986, last night, August, five months

Team A S1 : I've been out for two hours.
Team B S1 : I haven't seen him since last week.
Team A S2 : I haven't had a present since Christmas.
Team B S2 : I haven't worked for last summer.
Teacher : Wrong! I haven't worked since last summer. Team B doesn't get a point.

Oral Activity 17 (Talk about yourself)

Say what you have already done or not yet done today.
e.g. I've already tidied my room but I haven't washed the dishes yet.

Writing Activity 8

Write a letter to a friend with the latest news. Write what has happened and when it happened.

10. The Future (Will / Be Going To)

Is there any steak?
Yes sir, there is.
Is there any French wine?
Yes, we have excellent French wine sir.
Shall I give you the menu sir?
Yes, please!
What will you have for dinner sir?
We'll have some potatoes and green salad.
Will you have some wine with it?
No, thanks. We'll have some water, please.

Affirmative		Negative		Interrogative
Long form	**Short form**	**Long form**	**Short form**	
I **will** pay	I**'ll** pay	I **will not** pay	I **won't** pay	**Shall** I pay?
You will pay	You'll pay	You will not pay	You won't pay	Will you pay?
He will pay	He'll pay	He will not pay	He won't pay	Will he pay?
She will pay	She'll pay	She will not pay	She won't pay	Will she pay?
It will pay	It'll pay	It will not pay	It won't pay	Will it pay?
We will pay	We'll pay	We will not pay	We won't pay	Shall we pay?
You will pay	You'll pay	You will not pay	You won't pay	Will you pay?
They will pay	They'll pay	They will not pay	They won't pay	Will they pay?

126 Complete the sentences as in the example :

Long form	Short form
1. It .... *will* .... rain tomorrow.	It ..*'ll* .... rain tomorrow.
2. I hope you .... not be ill.	I hope you .... be ill.
3. He .... pass the test.	He .... pass the test.
4. We .... have a party.	We .... have a party.

We use the Future tense for actions which will happen in the future.

Time expressions used with the Future

tomorrow, tonight, soon, next week/month/year etc, in a week/month etc

Will	is used to express predictions, warnings, offers, promises, threats, requests, suggestions, on-the-spot decisions, opinions, hopes and fears (especially with words such as: think, expect, suppose, hope, believe, know and probably.)
Shall	can be used with "**I**" or "**We**" in questions, suggestions and offers.

127 Write the speech situations as in the example:

prediction, offer, warning, promise, threat, request, on-the-spot decision, fear

1. ..... *warning* ....

Don't eat all the cake.
You will be sick.

2. ....

I'll close the window.
It's very windy.

3. ....

Don't worry!
I'll buy you a new one.

4. ....

Shall I do the washing-up?

5. ....

Will you help me?

6. ....

BANK
Freeze or I'll shoot.

7. ....

You will soon be rich.

8. ....

I'm afraid you will get drunk.

9. ....

I will marry you soon.

128 Fill in "will" or "won't".

Johnny: Mum, 1) .... *will* .... I need to take my umbrella on holiday?
Mum: No, I don't think it 2) .... rain. Spain is a very hot country.
Johnny: 3) .... they speak English there?
Mum: No, they 4) .... speak English. They speak Spanish in Spain.
Johnny: 5) .... I like Spain, Mum?
Mum: I don't know Johnny. Maybe you 6) .... like it. Maybe you 7) ....
Johnny: Mum, I hope you 8) .... leave me there.
Mum: Stop asking so many questions or I 9) .... leave you there!

129 Fill in "will", "won't" or "shall".

Jim: 1) .... *Shall* .... we go to "Snacks" restaurant for lunch?
Mary: No, you 2) .... like the food there. I think you 3) .... like the new café in York Street.
Jim: O.K. We 4) .... take the bus there. 5) .... I phone John and ask him if he wants to come?
Mary: I'm sure he 6) .... want to come, but we 7) .... have time to wait for him here.
Jim: 8) .... I tell him to meet us there?
Mary: That's a good idea. Tell him we 9) .... meet him outside the café. There 10) .... be a lot of people so he 11) .... find us inside.
Jim: 12) .... I tell him to be there in half an hour? 13) .... that be enough time?
Mary: Yes, I think so.

130 Choose the correct item.

1. Do you think it .... *C* .... tomorrow?
   A) rained B) has rained C) will rain
2. Andy .... his horse three times a week.
   A) is riding B) has ridden C) rides
3. What an awful noise! What .... upstairs?
   A) have they done B) are they doing C) will they do
4. Take your umbrella or you .... wet.
   A) gets B) got C) will get
5. Look! It .... now.
   A) rained B) is raining C) has rained
6. .... you help me with the dishes?
   A) Will B) Shall C) Have
7. She .... to us yet.
   A) didn't write B) hasn't written C) doesn't write
8. He seldom .... his hair.
   A) washes B) wash C) has washed
9. Yesterday we .... a big cake and ate it all.
   A) have bought B) will buy C) bought
10. .... Sheila since her car accident?
    A) Will you see B)Did you see C)Have you seen
11. Dad .... to London at the moment.
    A) drove B) has driven C) is driving
12. They .... their homework an hour ago.
    A) will finish B) are finishing C) finished

"Will" versus "Be Going To"

Bye, I'll see you later.
Watch out! You're going to fall down that hole.
DANGER

Help! I'm going to faint.
I'll call an ambulance.
DANGER

"Will" is used	"Be going to" is used
1. to express on-the-spot decisions. It's cold. **I'll close** the window.	**1. to express things already decided in the near future.** **He is going to fly** to Rome tomorrow.
2. to express predictions, promises etc. **It will rain** tomorrow.	**2. to express intention.** He likes acting. **He is going to be** an actor.
3. when it is not certain that something will happen but it is just a prediction. If he comes early, **we will go** to the cinema.	**3. when there is evidence that something will definitely happen.** Watch out! **You're going to fall over.**

131 Match the sentences with the pictures, then write in the speech situations as in the example:

1) I like aeroplanes. I'm going to be a pilot.
2) It's very hot. I'll open the window.
3) She's going to have a bath.
4) I'll catch a cold if I go out tonight.
5) Get up or you will be late for work.
6) I've got a toothache. I'm going to see my dentist.

prediction, warning, intention, on-the-spot decision, evidence, something already decided

1. *something already decided*

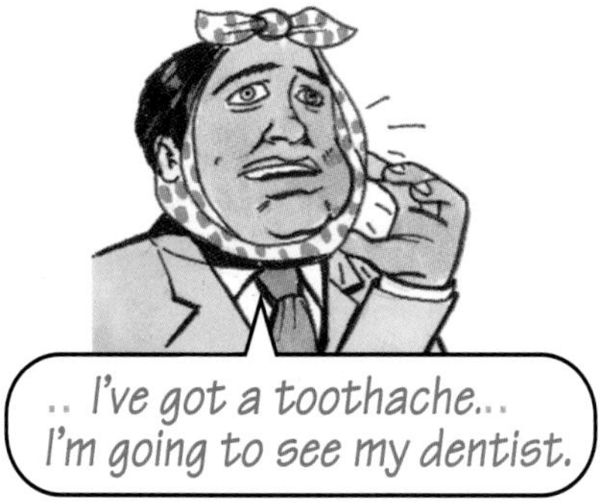

.. I've got a toothache...
I'm going to see my dentist.

2. ....

....
....

3. ....

....
....

4. ....

5. ....

6. ....

132 Fill in "will" or "be going to" in the correct form.

1. A: What do you want to do when you leave school?
   B: I *'m going to* .... be a dancer.
2. A: I think the house is on fire!
   B: I .... phone the fire brigade.
3. A: I'll get the sugar from the cupboard.
   B: Watch out! You .... hit your head on the door.
4. A: Haven't you finished those letters yet?
   B: No, I .... stay late and finish them.
5. A: .... you have another cake?
   B: No, thank you, I've already had two.
6. A: Do you want to go to the park this afternoon?
   B: I can't - I .... visit my grandparents.
7. A: This box is very heavy!
   B: I .... carry it for you.
8. A: .... you open the window, please?
   B: No, it's too cold in here.
9. A: Have you bought a birthday present for Sally?
   B: Yes. I .... give her a box of chocolates.
10. A: I've lost my pen.
    B: I .... give you one of mine.
11. A: Have you seen Sue today?
    B: No, but I expect she .... telephone me tonight.
12. A: Put your money in your pocket or you .... lose it.
    B: It's O.K. It's safer in my bag.
13. A: Have you decided what to study at university?
    B: Yes, I .... study Biology.
14. A: Do you want to borrow my car?
    B: Thanks. I .... bring it back tonight.
15. A: The house is very dirty!
    B: I know. I .... clean it this afternoon.

133 Look at the pictures and write sentences using the "be going to" form, "Present Continuous" or "Present Perfect".

1. (She / wash hair) .. *She's* .. . *going to wash her hair.*
2. .... *She's washing* .... *her hair.* ....
3. ..... *She has washed* .... *her hair.* ....

4. (He / study) ....
5. ....
6. ....

7. (He / cook) ....
8. ....
9. ....

134 Choose the correct item.

1. Julie .... *B* .... me since September.
   A) isn't going to visit   B) hasn't visited   C) won't visit

2. If he doesn't hurry, he .... the bus.
   A) has missed   B) is going to miss   C) will miss

3. .... the bus to school every day?
   A) Are you taking   B) Do you take   C) Have you taken

4. They .... on holiday with us last year.
   A) came   B) have come   C) are going to come

5. I .... Pat at 7 o'clock tonight.
   A) have seen   B) see   C) am going to see

Oral Activity 18

The teacher divides the class into two teams and writes cues on the board. Then he/she invites his/her students to say what they will do or won't do when they are parents. Each correct sentence gets 1 point. The team with the most points is the winner. The teacher starts the game first.

Cues: **go to parties, drink wine/ beer, buy them presents, take them to the cinema, have bad friends, hit them, play with them, help them with their schoolwork, go to bed late, watch TV, shout at them, make them cry etc.**

Teacher: When I am a parent I will love my children.
Team A S1: When I am a parent I won't let my children go to parties.
Team B S1: When I am a parent I .... (no answer) etc.
Team A gets 1 point but Team B doesn't get a point.

Oral Activity 19 (Fortune-telling)

Your students work in pairs and tell each other his / her fortune by looking at his/her palm.

e.g. You will win a lot of money. You will meet a millionaire. etc.

Writing Activity 9

Write what you will be doing in twenty years' time. How old will you be? What will you be? Where will you live? Will you be married? etc.

Oral Activity 20

The teacher divides the class into two teams and chooses a leader. He/she gives the leader a piece of paper which says what he/she is going to do tomorrow. The teams ask questions in turn until they find out what the leader is going to do. Each correct guess gets 1 point. The team with the most points is the winner.

Leader's list: **do the shopping, watch TV, do homework, stay up late, visit grandparents, play tennis etc.**

Team A S1: Are you going to play golf?
Leader: No, I'm not.
Team B S1: Are you going to play tennis?
Leader: Yes, I am.

Team A S2: Are you going to watch TV?
Leader: Yes, I am.
Team B S2: Are you going to write a letter?
Leader: No, I'm not. etc

Writing Activity 10

Write what you are going to do each day next week.

Example: On Monday ..... I'm going to meet my friends and go to the park. ....
On Tuesday ....
On Wednesday .... etc.

11. Yes / No questions — Wh- questions

1. Questions are usually formed by changing the word order; this means the auxiliary or modal verb comes before the subject. (Auxiliary / modal verbs are : can, have, be, will, shall, must)	**Is she** happy? **Can she** type? **Have you** ever been to Paris? **Will you** help me? **Shall we** go out tonight?
2. In the Present Simple, questions are formed by using do / does and in the Past Simple by using did.	**Do you like** sweets? **Does he** often **visit** them? **Did he pass** the test?
3. Wh - questions start with a question word : who, where, what, when, why, how, which etc.	**Who** did you go out with? **Where** did you meet her? **What** is your name?

135 You are interviewing a famous actor. He tells you some things but you want to know more.

1. I like reading books (What). ...... *What books do you like reading?*..............................
2. I like spaghetti (pizza). .... *Do you like pizza too?*..............................
3. I go to the gym to keep fit (How often). ....
4. I can dance very well (sing). ....
5. I play musical instruments (What). ....
6. I never get up early (What time). ....
7. I visited Paris last year (London). ....
8. I've got an expensive house (car). ....
9. I buy expensive clothes (Where). ....
10. I'm going on a tour of Europe soon (Japan). ....
11. I live in America (Where). ....
12. I go to parties (How often). ....

We normally use question words for :

people	jobs / things / animals / actions	place	time	quantity	manner	reason
Who Whose Which (one of)	What Which (one of)	Where	When How long What time How often	How much How many	How	Why

136 Fill in "When", "How", "How old", "How many", "Where", "Who", "What time" or "Which".

1. .... *How many* ..... pets have you got? Two.
2. .... is your birthday? 12th June.
3. .... do you work? In a hospital.
4. .... are you? I'm fine thanks!
5. .... does she feel? She's ill.
6. .... sisters have you got? One.
7. .... do you get to work? By bus.
8. .... does the bus leave? At 8.00.
9. .... does the washing-up? My brother and I do.
10. .... are you going? To the cinema.
11. .... biscuits would you like? These ones, please!
12. .... are you? Ten years old.

Subject questions

If who, which or what are the subject of the question, we do not put the verb in question form.

subject		object
Harry	loves	Jane.

Who loves Jane? (Not who ~~does~~ love ...)

subject		object
Jane	loves	**Bob.**

Who does Jane love?

137 Make questions for the following sentences.

1. Who ...... *came late last night* .... ?	John came late last night.
2. Where .... ?	Fish live in the water.
3. What .... ?	Birds fly in the air.
4. Who .... ?	John telephoned a week ago.
5. When .... ?	John telephoned a week ago.
6. Which of you .... ?	All of us want to help.
7. Who .... to her?	John and Sue sent a letter to her.
8. What .... ?	They sent her some flowers.
9. Who .... Sue?	Paul invited Sue.
10. Who .... Ann .... ?	Ann met Tony.
11. Which dress .... ?	She bought the red dress.

138 Write questions to which the bold type words are the answers.

His name is **John Page**. He's from **Portsmouth, England**. He is **a bank clerk**. He's **24 years old**. He's got **one sister**. His sister's name is **Sarah**. He likes **rock music and heavy metal**. His favourite group is "**Iron Maiden**".

1. .... *What is his name?* ....
2. ....
3. ....
4. ....
5. ....
6. ....
7. ....
8. ....

139 Fill in "why", "what", "which", "who", "how often" or "where".

Inspector : Will you answer some questions, please?
Suspect : 1) .... *What* .... do you want to know?
Inspector : 2) .... were you at 10 o'clock last night?
Suspect : I was at the cinema.
Inspector : 3) .... cinema were you at?
Suspect : "The Embassy" in Temple Street.
Inspector : And 4) .... was the film that you saw?
Suspect : I can't remember what it was called, I'm afraid.
Inspector : 5) .... did you go with?
Suspect : No one. I went on my own.
Inspector : 6) .... do you go to the cinema?
Suspect : Not very often. I prefer the theatre.
Inspector : So 7) .... did you decide to go yesterday?
Suspect : It was a film I've always wanted to see.
Inspector : Then 8) .... can't you remember what it was called?

140 Ask the questions to which the bold type words are the answers.

Tom has been in London **for two years**. He studies **at the university**. He wants to be **a lawyer**. He lives **in a small flat**. It belongs to **his uncle, Lucas**. Tonight, **his friend Tony** has invited Tom to a party. **Tony's** sister is getting engaged to Steve Johnson, a friend of theirs. **Steve** works with Tony as a shop assistant. Tom is going to meet Susan at Victoria Station **at 8.00**. He must be there on time **because if he isn't, Susan will be angry with him**. **Tom** likes Susan but Susan likes **Tony**.

1. .. *How long has Tom been in London* .. ? .... *For two years.* ...
2. .... ? ....
3. .... ? ....
4. .... ? ....
5. .... ? ....
6. .... ? ....
7. .... ? ....
8. .... ? ....
9. .... ? ....
10. .... ? ....
11. .... ? ....
12. .... ? ....

141 Complete the reporter's interview with Susan Star's assistant.

R: 1) *What time does Susan wake up?* .....
S: Susan wakes up at 9 o'clock.
R: 2) ....
S: She has breakfast in bed.
R: 3) ....
S: She starts work at 11 o'clock.
R: 4) ....
S: No, she goes to work by taxi.
R: 5) ....
S: Yes, she works in Hollywood.
R: 6) ....
S: Yes, she usually goes to bed late.
R: 7) ....
S: She lives with her mother.
R: 8) ....
S: No, she isn't married.
R: 9) ....
S: Two sisters and one brother.
R: 10) ....
S: Their names are Helen, Mary and John.

142 Choose the correct word.

1. ..... C ...... did you buy that skirt? Last week.
   A) Who B) Where C) When
2. .... is the black car? John's.
   A) Who B) Whose C) Which
3. .... do you travel abroad? Every year.
   A) How many B) How C) How often
4. .... is your name? Ted.
   A) Where B) Why C) What
5. ....are you? Nine.
   A) How old B) How long C) How much
6. .... are you late? I overslept.
   A) Why B) Who C) How
7. .... is John? He's upstairs.
   A) Who B) Where C) What
8. .... is the Philips TV? £150.
   A) How B) How many C) How much
9. .... have you been here? Two weeks.
   A) How long B) How much C) How many
10. .... is your car? The white one.
   A) Which B) When C) Whose

143 Complete the reporter's questions.

Reporter : 1) .... What is your real name............. ?
Spike Sparkle : My real name is Eric Stanley Smith.
Reporter : 2) .... ?
Spike Sparkle : I was twelve years old when I first started singing.
Reporter : 3) .... ?
Spike Sparkle : I made my first record in 1988.
Reporter : 4) .... ?
Spike Sparkle : I live in the centre of London.
Reporter : 5) .... ?
Spike Sparkle : Paris is my favourite city.
Reporter : 6) .... ?
Spike Sparkle : I go there three times a year.
Reporter : 7) .... ?
Spike Sparkle : In my Rolls Royce or my private plane.
Reporter : 8) .... ?
Spike Sparkle : I like Elvis Presley and the Rolling Stones.
Reporter : 9) .... ?

Spike Sparkle : I earn lots and lots!
Reporter : 10) .... ?
Spike Sparkle : My mother is my favourite person.
Reporter : 11) .... ?
Spike Sparkle : I'll be here for two weeks.

Oral Activity 21 (Guessing Game)

The teacher divides the class into two teams and chooses a leader. The leader chooses a person from page 80.The two teams in turn try to guess who he is by asking the leader wh- questions.

Team A S1: Where is he from? Leader: He is from Germany.

Team B S1: How old is he?
Leader: He's 23.
Team A S2: What's his favourite sport?
Leader: Swimming.
Team B S2: What kind of music does he like?
Leader: Classical music.
Team A S3: Is it Walter?
Leader: Yes, it's Walter.

Team A wins. Choose a new leader and play the game again.

Frank	David	Paul	Walter	Pierre
Germany	**Scotland**	**France**	**Germany**	**France**
student	teacher	taxi driver	student	taxi driver
23	28	21	23	21
1 brother	1 sister	1 sister	1 brother	1 brother
swimming	sailing	skiing	swimming	climbing
pop music	pop music	jazz	classical music	jazz

Jose	Gonzales	Eric	Michel	Andrew
Spain	**Spain**	**Germany**	**France**	**Scotland**
bank clerk	bank clerk	doctor	taxi driver	engineer
24	24	28	21	28
2 sisters	2 brothers	1 brother	1 sister	1 sister
football	football	swimming	climbing	sailing
classical music	classical music	pop music	pop music	classical music

Writing Activity 11

Imagine that you are a reporter. Write an interview you had with a famous person.

12. Prepositions of Place - Movement - Time

144 **First read the text, then cover it, look at the picture and answer the questions that follow.**

The Greens live **in** a very beautiful cottage. Mrs Green is looking **out of** the sitting room window. Mr Green is going **through** the front door **into** the cottage. **Outside** the cottage there's a garden. There are some children playing **in** the garden. Bill is climbing **up** a tree and Jane is sliding **down** a slide. **Inside** the kennel there's Butch, their dog. **Next to** the kennel Ann is climbing **onto** a swing. Timmy, the cat, is walking **along by** the wall **towards** the garden shed. Grandpa is standing **at** the shed door.

1. Where do the Greens live? .... *In a very beautiful cottage.* ....
2. What is Mrs Green doing? ....
3. Where is Mr Green going? ....
4. Where's the garden? ....
5. Where are the children? ....
6. Where is Bill climbing? ....
7. Where is Jane sliding? ....
8. Where's Butch? ....
9. Where's Ann? ....
10. Where is Ann climbing? ....
11. Where is Timmy walking? ....
12. Where is Grandpa standing? ....

145 First read the text, then cover it, look at the picture and answer the questions that follow.

Mr Lawson has parked his car **in front of** the garage **beside** the house. He has got out of the car and he's walking **towards** the house. He is holding something **behind** his back. Oh! It's a bunch of flowers. Mrs Lawson is standing **by** the front door smiling. It's their wedding anniversary today.

1. Where has Mr Lawson parked his car? .... *In front of the garage.* ....
2. Where's the garage? ....
3. Where's he walking? ....
4. Where's he holding the bunch of flowers? ....
5. Where's Mrs Lawson standing? ....

146 First read the text, then cover it, look at the picture and answer the questions that follow.

I am going **from** London **to** Plymouth on a train. I'm sitting **next to** my friend John. Two old ladies are sitting **opposite** us. My travel bag is **in** the rack **above** my head. John has his suitcase **under** his seat. There's a table **between** our seats and the old ladies' seats. There's a puppy **under** the table. A ticket-inspector is coming down the train. Oh no! Where's my ticket?

1. Where are you going? .... *From London to Plymouth.* ....
2. Where are you sitting? ....
3. Where are the two old ladies sitting? ....
4. Where's your bag? ....
5. Where's John's suitcase? ....
6. Where's the table? ....
7. Where's the puppy? ....
8. Where's your ticket? ....

147 First explain the prepositions in the box. Then fill in the blanks with the correct preposition. Finally, cover the text and describe the scene in the picture.

towards, in front of, out of, into, across, along, over, round, next to

The High Street is busy on Saturdays. A policeman is walking 1) .... *across* .... the street. He is going 2) .... the bank. Two women are going 3) .... the bank. A man is coming 4) .... the café 5) .... the bank. There is a boy standing 6) .... the toyshop. A toy aeroplane is flying 7) .... the boy's head and he is watching it. Two girls are running 8) .... the street. They're trying to catch a bus but the bus is disappearing 9) .... the corner.

148 Look at the picture and fill in "on", "at", "opposite", "beside", "in", "behind", "under", "next to" or "above".

It is Ann's sixteenth birthday and she is having a party 1) ..*at*.. her house. There is a long table 2) .... the wall with lots of food and drinks 3) .... it. 4) .... it there is a sign which says "Happy Birthday". A few young men are standing 5) .... the table with glasses 6) .... their hands. 7) .... the table is a stereo with some cassettes and records 8) .... it. Some girls are dancing 9) .... the room. Someone is standing 10) .... Ann with a present 11) .... his arm.

Study these idiomatic usages:

by car (but in my car)	by taxi (but in a taxi)	by boat	go to work (but go on holiday)
by helicopter (but in a helicopter)	by bus (but on / in a bus)	by sea	in Athens (but at Athens airport)
by train (but on a train)	by air	on foot	on a chair (but in an armchair)
by plane (but on the plane)	by ship	in danger	at the bus-stop

149 Fill in the correct prepositions.

Jack Smithers, the famous British secret agent, was 1) .... *on* .... holiday in Scotland when he got a message. "Some terrorists are sending guns from America to Africa 2) .... ship. Your job is to stop them." Jack decided to go to the airport 3) .... helicopter and not 4) .... his car. He was 5) .... Glasgow airport, sitting 6) .... a chair waiting for his flight to New York, when he saw one of the terrorists. It was clear that the terrorists had a different plan, and wanted to carry the guns 7) .... plane. Jack had to do something fast or the people 8) .... the plane would be 9) .... danger. The plane was full of people going 10) .... summer holiday. What could he do?

Prepositions of Time

She wakes up
at 6 o'clock in the morning.

He sleeps late
on Sunday.

She goes on holiday
at Easter or in summer.

in	at	on
in the morning	at 8 o'clock	on Fridays
in the afternoon	at noon	on Wednesday
in the evening	at night	on Thursday (days) etc.
in August (months)	at midnight	on January 27th (dates)
in summer (seasons)	at Easter	on Monday morning
in 1992 (years)	at Christmas	on a cold day
in the 20th century	at the weekend	on a summer night

150 Fill in "at", "on" or "in".

1. .... *In* .... September
2. .... March 25th
3. .... the afternoon
4. 1983
5. .... Friday
6. .... the evening
7. .... 9 o'clock
8. .... a hot day
9. .... Christmas
10. .... spring
11. .... New Year's Day
12. .... 10 o'clock
13. .... midnight
14. .... Sundays
15. .... Easter
16. .... the 19th century
17. .... Saturday night
18. .... night
19. .... noon
20. .... the weekend
21. .... a summer day
22. .... Friday morning
23. .... autumn
24. .... a winter night

151 Complete the sentences with "in", "on" or "at".

1. Christmas is ... *on* .... the 25th of December.
2. It's cold .... winter.
3. I always have a nap .... the afternoon.
4. My birthday is .... October.
5. She left late .... night.
6. Sue's party is .... 4 o'clock .... Friday.
7. We watch cartoons on TV .... the evening.
8. It's hot .... summer.
9. He woke up late .... the morning.
10. She moved house .... 1989.
11. We usually don't go out .... Mondays.
12. It's windy .... autumn.
13. Her daughter was born .... August 2nd.
14. They got married .... July.

152 Fill in: "in", "on" or "at".

1) ..... *At* .... Christmas, our family has a good time. We always have a party 2) .... the 24th of December. 3) .... the afternoon we make pies and 4) .... night the party starts. People start to arrive 5) .... 9 o'clock. 6) .... midnight, we all sing "We Wish You a Merry Christmas". Christmas Day is 7) .... the 25th of December. 8) .... the morning we open our presents and 9) .... 2 o'clock we have "Christmas dinner". My favourite Christmas was 10) .... 1990. We visited our uncle in Australia. Christmas is 11) .... summer there. We had our Christmas dinner on the beach 12) .... the afternoon.

153 Fill in: "in", "on" or "at".

1) . *At* .. the weekend Peter is very busy. 2) .... Saturdays he gets up 3) .... 7 o'clock and he goes for a walk with his dog. They come home 4) .... 8 o'clock and he has breakfast. 5) .... the morning Peter does his homework, then he has lunch 6) .... 1 o'clock. 7) .... 4 o'clock he goes swimming with his friends. 8) .... the winter they go to the swimming pool, but 9) .... the summer they can swim in the sea. 10) .... about 5.30 they say "goodbye" and go home. 11) .... the evening Peter watches TV. His favourite programme is the sports programme 12) .... 8.30 13) .... Saturday evenings. 14) .... Sundays, he tidies his room, digs the garden and he sometimes goes to the cinema.

154 Fill in : "at", "beside", "in", "behind", "on", "opposite", "from ... to", "above" or "in front of".

Mary is 1) . at .. the airport. She's waiting for her flight 2) .... Athens 3) .... London. There's a man sitting 4) .... her. He's got a cap 5) .... his head. There are some suitcases 6) .... them. An old woman is sleeping 7) .... the seat 8) .... them. 9) .... Mary there's a security guard. He's got a walkie-talkie 10) .... his hand. 11) .... him there's the information board.

Oral Activity 22

The teacher divides the class into two teams. Then he / she says expressions of time without their prepositions. The teams in turn should give the missing prepositions. The teams get 1 point for each correct answer. The team with the most points is the winner.

Teacher: spring
Team A S1: in spring
Teacher: 1992
Team B S1: at 1992
Teacher: Wrong! It's **in** 1992. Team B doesn't get a point.

Oral Activity 23

The teacher divides the class into two teams and chooses a leader. The leader thinks of an object in the classroom. The teams in turn try to find out where the object is by asking questions using prepositions. The team which finds where the object is first is the winner.

Leader: (chair behind T's desk)
Team A S1: Is it under the chair?
Leader: No, it isn't.
Team B S1: Is it on the wall?
Leader: No, it isn't.
Team A S2: Is it on the T's desk?
Leader: No, it isn't.
Team B S2: Is it behind the T's desk?
Leader: Yes, it is. It's the chair.

Team B is the winner. The teacher chooses another leader and you play the game again.

Writing Activity 12

Find a magazine picture and write the positions of the people and the objects in it.

Revision Exercises III

155 Choose the correct item.

1. Next Sunday .... A .... the National Museum.
   A) I'm going to visit B) I visit C) I haven't visited

2. We usually open our gifts ..... Christmas Day.
   A) at B) on C) in

3. There is very ..... soap left. I must buy some.
   A) few B) little C) a little

4. Have you seen my pen .... ?
   A) somewhere B) nowhere C) anywhere

5. Is this record .... ?
   A) your B) you C) yours

6. I haven't corrected the tests ....
   A) just B) since C) yet

7. .... do you visit your dentist?
   A) How much B) How often C) How many

8. When I was young I .... in a village.
   A) have lived B) am living C) lived

9. Ted is standing .... the bus-stop.
   A) on B) at C) in

10. Fred .... in the office ten minutes ago.
    A) wasn't B) won't be C) hasn't been

11. They haven't seen her .... last Tuesday.
    A) yet B) for C) since

12. There is .... Coke in the bottle. Do you want some?
    A) a little B) a few C) little

13. Ann has .... come home from school.
    A) yet B) already C) since

14. My grandfather ... on the sofa at the moment.
    A) lies B) is lying C) has lain

15. .... I help you with the dishes?
    A) Will B) Shall C) Am I going

16. The waiter brought us three .... of beer.
    A) jars B) bottles C) cartons

17. My father can drive but he .... a car.
    A) didn't get B) doesn't get C) hasn't got

18. This one is his and that one is ....
    A) she B) her C) hers

19. Victor wants .... accordion for his birthday.
    A) – B) a C) an

20. I think there are .... behind the cupboard.
    A) mouses B) mice C) mices

21. We haven't got .... money.
    A) many B) little C) much

22. Does .... know the answer?
    A) no one B) someone C) anyone

23. At the moment Mick .... his new car.
    A) is driving B) drives C) will drive

24. Mother .... some cheese.
    A) is needing B) needs C) need

25. How long .... in New York?
    A) have you been B) are you C) did you go

26. Do you like milk? Yes, I ....
    A) like B) am C) do

27. ....father is a footballer.
    A) Their B) They're C) They

28. They .... go to school on Sunday.
    A) doesn't B) don't C) aren't

29. .... ate all the sweets.
    A) Nowhere B) Anyone C) Someone

30. Has he got a dog? Yes, he ....
    A) is B) has C) does

156 Find the mistake and correct it.

1. ~~Will~~ I help you with the cooking? ...... *Shall* .....
2. She has worked here since a month. ....
3. We bought some new furnitures yesterday. ....
4. There isn't no one in the room. ....
5. I left for Paris at 10:00 tomorrow. ....
6. Want you some ice-cream? ....
7. Kim hasn't got much friends. ....
8. It often is cold in December. ....
9. We didn't went on holiday last summer. ....
10. Brian just left. ....

157 Put the verbs in brackets into "Present Simple" or "Present Continuous".

Every summer Tonia and her family 1) .... *go* .... (go) on holiday. They usually 2) .... (stay) in England but at the moment they 3) .... (travel) by plane. They 4) .... (go) to America! Tonia 5) .... (be) very excited. She 6) .... (look) out of the window and she 7) .... (laugh). Her brother 8) .... (play) a game. He 9) .... (like) aeroplanes. He 10) .... (want) to be a pilot when he grows up.

158 Put the verbs in brackets into "Past Simple".

Last week we 1) ...... *drove* ...... (drive) to London. It 2) .... (be) a beautiful day. When we 3) .... (get) there, we 4) .... (park) the car and 5) .... (catch) the tube into the centre of town. We 6) .... (go) to Oxford Street and 7) .... (spend) a lot of money in the shops. In the afternoon we 8) .... (see) the Changing of the Guard outside Buckingham Palace. There 9) .... (be) many people there and everybody 10) .... (wave) at the Guards. Later we 11) .... (have) a boat ride down the Thames. We 12) .... (eat) our dinner on the boat and then we 13) .... (decide) to go home. We all 14) .... (sleep) on the journey home except Dad.

159 Put the verbs in brackets into "Present Perfect" or "Past Simple".

a. Tom : 1) .... *Have you ever been* .... (you / ever / be) to Paris?
Jack : Yes, I have. I 2) .... (go) there last year.
Tom : What 3) .... (you / see)?
Jack : I 4) .... (see) the Eiffel Tower and 5) .... (visit) the Louvre.

b. Tim : 1) .... (you / ever / be) to an art gallery?
John : Yes, I 2) .... (be) at the National Gallery yesterday.
Tim : 3) .... (you / like) it?
John : Yes, it 4) .... (be) nice. Actually, it's the first time I 5) .... (ever / visit) an art gallery.

160 Find the mistakes and correct them.

1) Today ~~was~~ Monday. 2) John and Harry is at school. 3) They sit at their desks at the moment. 4) John looks at the teacher. 5) She writes on the board. 6) John like Maths. 7) He is bringing his homework every day 8) and he never is late for school. 9) His brother Harry not like Maths. 10) At the moment he talks to his friend.

1. ...... *is* .... 3. .... 5. .... 7. .... 9. ....
2. .... 4. .... 6. .... 8. .... 10. ....

161 Put the verbs in brackets into "Present Simple" or "Present Continuous".

We 1) .... *are* ..... (be) in the playground. We 2) .... (have) a break at the moment. Some children 3) .... (play) hide-and-seek. I 4) .... (sit) on a bench. I usually 5) .... (eat) a sandwich but today I 6) .... (drink) Coke. My friend 7) .... (eat) a big bag of crisps. Our teacher 8) .... (walk) around the playground. She always 9) .... (watch) us or 10) .... (play) with us. We all 11) .... (love) her.

162 Put the verbs in brackets into the "Present Perfect" or "Past Simple".

a. Jenny: Julie, 1) .... *have you ever driven* .... (you / ever / drive) a car?
Julie: No, but I 2) .... (drive) a tractor.
Jenny: Where 3) .... (you / drive) it?
Julie: I 4) .... (drive) it on my uncle's farm.

b. Peter: Bobbie, 5) .... (you / ever / see) a ghost?
Bobbie: No, but I 6) .... (see) a UFO.
Peter: Where 7) .... (you / see) it?
Bobbie: I 8) .... (see) it in a field.

163 Fill in "for", "since", "already", "yet" or "just".

1. I've .... *already* ...... seen this film twice.
2. Hasn't she come .... ?
3. She hasn't cleaned her room ....
4. He hasn't written to us .... last month.
5. We haven't been out .... a week.
6. Mr Smith has .... called you.
7. I haven't seen him .... Monday.
8. Mother has .... cooked dinner.
9. He has been in Dublin .... March.
10. We haven't been to the cinema .... ages.
11. Haven't you finished .... ?
12. She has .... got her test results.

164 Look at the picture and the verb list, then write what they're going to do, they're doing or they have done.

make, welcome, eat, play, listen, cry, take, watch, arrive

1. Mother .... has made a cake. ....
2. The Greens' friends ....
3. Father ....
4. The cats ....
5. The boy and the girl ....
6. Grandfather ....
7. Grandmother ....
8. The baby ....
   because the dog .... his ball.

165 Fill in "on", "at", or "in".

Mr Bell wanted to go somewhere warm and sunny 1) .... at .... Easter. 2) .... April 25th he flew to Greece early 3) .... the morning. He arrived 4) .... Athens airport 5) .... 6 o'clock and drove directly to his friends' village. He reached the village 6) .... 2 o'clock 7) .... the afternoon. 8) .... Sunday he ate a wonderful traditional lunch. 9) .... the evening he went out with his friends and met lots of new people. They returned home 10) .... midnight and went to bed. He flew back home to England 11) .... April 29th.

166 Fill in "what", "how long", "why", "how", "how much", "how many", "where" or "when".

A: Good morning.
B: Good morning Mr Jones, please sit down. I need some information. 1) .... What .... are your qualifications?
A: I have a Chemistry Degree.
B: 2) .... old are you?
A: I'm 27 years old.
B: 3) .... did you study?
A: In London.
B: 4) .... do you work now?
A: At ABC Chemicals.
B: 5) .... have you worked there?
A: For three years.
B: 6) .... do you want to leave?
A: I want a more interesting job.
B: 7) .... do you earn there?
A: £30,000 a year.
B: 8) .... weeks' holiday do you get?
A: Four weeks a year.
B: Oh, I see, and 9) .... can you leave your job?
A: In two weeks' time.
B: And 10) .... job would you like to do here?
A: I'd like to work in the Sales Department.
B: Well, that's all the information we need.

167 Fill in "be going to" or "will" in the appropriate form.

Jill: 1) .... *Are you going to* .... make any New Year's Resolutions?
Jack: Yes, I 2) .... learn to drive.
Jill: Really! I 3) .... give you some lessons if you like. Have you got a car?
Jack: No, but I 4) .... start saving now and I expect I 5) .... buy one in the summer.
Jill: I 6) .... start learning Spanish and, if I can, I 7) .... go to Spain next year.
Jack: 8) .... you go alone?
Jill: No, I 9) .... probably ask some friends to come.

168 Fill in : "on", "in front of", "opposite", "beside", "under", "above", "in", "next to", "at" or "over".

This is Tom's study. Tom is sitting 1) .. *on* .. a chair 2) .... his desk. There's a map 3) .... the wall 4) .... his desk. His schoolbag is 5) .... the floor 6) .... the desk. 7) .... the desk there are some books. 8) .... the books there are some notebooks. 9) .... them there's a glass. There are pens and pencils 10) .... the glass. There are some bookshelves 11) .... the table. The table is 12) .... the door. There's a rug 13) .... the table.

169 Fill in the blanks with "someone", "anyone", "no one", "something", "anything" or "nothing".

It's a very hot day and there are many people on the beach. 1) .. *Someone* .. is swimming in the sea and there is 2) .... in the distance - I think it's a boat. 3) .... is putting on suntan cream but 4) .... is playing football. I can't see 5) .... eating ice-cream but 6) .... is eating an apple. There is 7) .... hiding under a towel - is it a dog? There is a large beach bag on the sand but there is 8) .... inside it. I can't see 9) .... wearing a hat but 10) .... is wearing sunglasses. Can you see 11)........................... else in the picture?

13. The Imperative

1. We use the Imperative when we tell one or more persons to do something. We normally use the Imperative for orders, warnings and instructions and for requests to people we know well. For more polite requests we use "could I", "could you", "would you".
2. "Let's" is used as a kind of Imperative for "we". We use "Let's" for suggestions.
3. We use "Don't" for the negative form of the Imperative.

170 Match the sentences with the pictures, then spot the speech situations.

Look out!	Be quiet! Don't talk!	Give me some bread, please!
Let's dance!	Let's play football!	Could I have some water, please?
Don't take photographs!	Don't walk on the grass!	Would you help me, please?

request, order, warning, suggestion, instruction, polite request

1. .... *request* ....
2. ....
3. ....

.. *Give me some bread,* .
...... *please!* ....

....
....

....
....

4. ....

5. ....

6. ....

7. ....

8. ....

9. ....

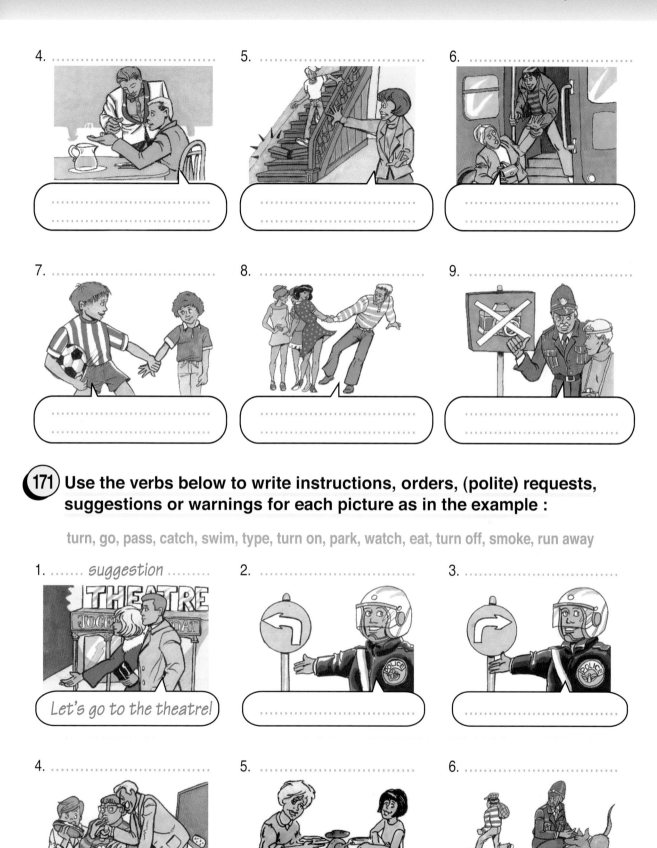

171 Use the verbs below to write instructions, orders, (polite) requests, suggestions or warnings for each picture as in the example :

turn, go, pass, catch, swim, type, turn on, park, watch, eat, turn off, smoke, run away

1. .... *suggestion* ....

Let's go to the theatre!

2. ....

3. ....

4. ....

5. ....

6. ....

7. ....

8. ....

9. ....

10. ....

11. ....

12. ....

13. ....

14. ....

15. ....

Oral Activity 24

The teacher divides the class into two teams. The teams in turn give each other orders. Each correct performance of the order gets 1 point.The team with the most points is the winner.

Team A S1 : Ann, stand up!
(Ann stands up.)

Team B S1 : Costas, turn off the light!
(Costas turns off the light.)

Team A S2 : Tony, open the door!
(Tony opens the door.)

Team B S2 : Maria, clean the board!
(Maria writes on the board.)

Teacher : Wrong! Team A doesn't get a point.

Writing Activity 13

Write down instructions for how to make an omelette. Here is a list of verbs to help you:

put, mix, add, beat, cook, break, pour

14. Adjectives / Adverbs / Comparisons

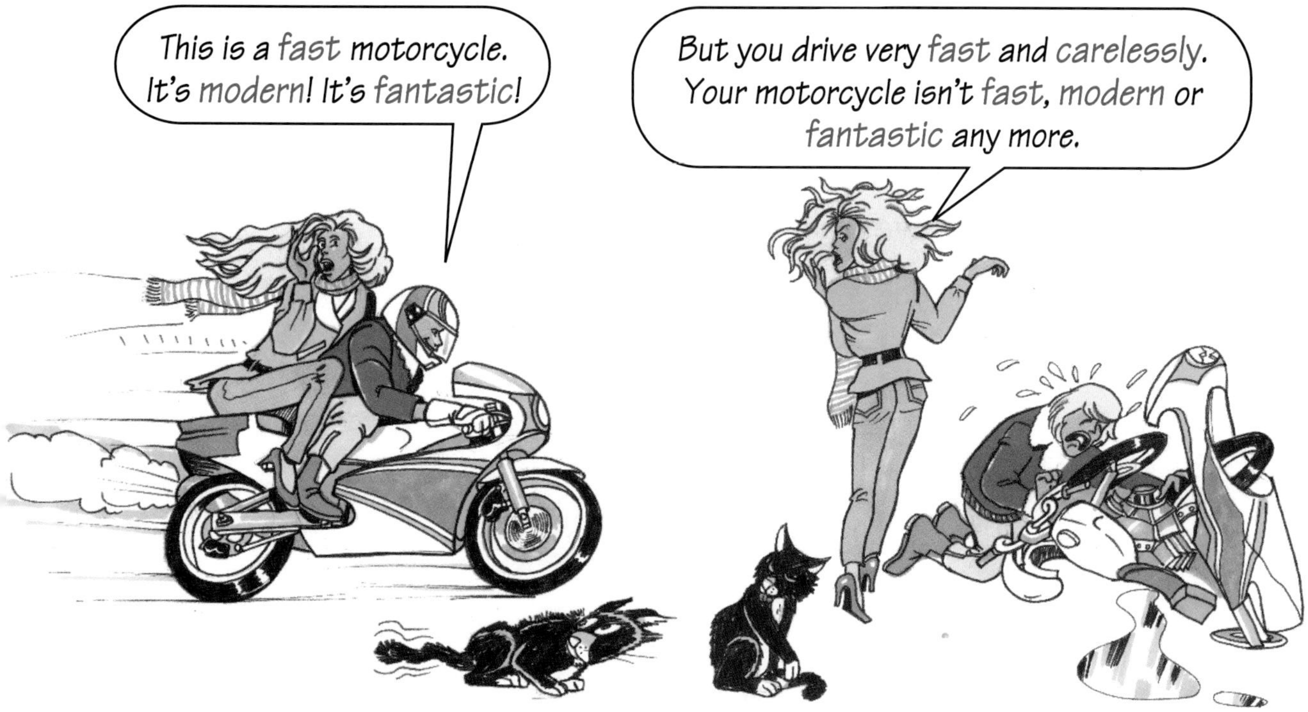

This is a fast motorcycle. It's modern! It's fantastic!
But you drive very fast and carelessly. Your motorcycle isn't fast, modern or fantastic any more.

Adjectives describe nouns. They say what something is like. Adjectives come before nouns or after "be". They have the same form in the singular and plural.

This is a **nice** dress. (What's the dress like? Nice.)	This train is **slow**. (What's the train like? Slow.)	These trains are **slow**. (NOT slows)

Adverbs describe verbs. They say how, where, when, how often someone does something.

He left the room **quickly**. (**How** did he leave the room? **Quickly**.)
She telephoned Jim **yesterday**. (**When** did she telephone Jim? **Yesterday**.)

Formation of Adverbs

We usually form an adverb by adding -ly to an adjective. **bad** **badly**

Adjectives ending in -le drop e and take -y.	Adjective	**simple** **terrible**	Adverb	**simply** **terribly**
Adjectives ending in consonant + y drop y and take -ily.	Adjective	**merry** **angry**	Adverb	**merrily** **angrily**

These adverbs are irregular:

Adjective	good	fast	hard	He's a **good** dancer. He dances **well**.
Adverb	well	fast	hard	He's a **hard** worker. He works **hard**.

172 Fill in the appropriate adverb.

1. nice .... nicely ....
2. angry ....
3. quiet ....
4. good ....
5. simple ....
6. careful ....
7. slow ....
8. easy ....
9. quick ....
10. comfortable ....
11. polite ....
12. happy ....

173 Choose an adjective from the list to fill in the blanks.

beautiful / ugly, tall / short, interesting / boring, quiet / noisy,
old / young, thin / fat, heavy / light, clean / dirty, old / new

1. ... heavy ....

2. ... light ....

3. ....

4. ....

5. ....

6. ....

7. ....

8. ....

9. ....

10. ....

11. ....

12. ....

13. ....

14. ....

15. ....

16. ....

17. ....

18. ....

174 Choose an adjective from the list to fill in the correct opposite.

little, fast, small, short, stupid, cold, sad, easy, thin

big

1. ... little....

thick

2. ....

long

3. ....

happy 4. .... large 5. .... slow 6. ....

     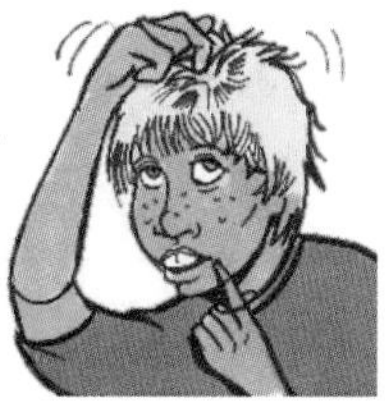

difficult 7. .... hot 8. .... clever 9. ....

175 Write what the underlined word is; adjective or adverb.

1. Fast runners win races. .... adjective ....
2. Mathematics is difficult. ....
3. She's a good pianist. ....
4. She behaved rudely to her boss. ....
5. You've done well in your test. ....
6. The clowns are very funny. ....
7. She's a pretty girl. ....
8. He runs fast. ....
9. Ann is very sad. ....
10. She plays the piano beautifully. ....
11. Father is very busy in his office. ....
12. The doctor arrived immediately. ....

176 Underline the correct item.

1. He left the room quiet / quietly.
2. Jane works hard / hardly.
3. He's a very nice / nicely man.
4. The sun is shining bright / brightly.
5. Smoking is bad / badly for your health.
6. She behaves very good / well.
7. He always dresses smart / smartly.
8. He shouted angry / angrily at me.
9. This chair is comfortable / comfortably.
10. He smiled sad / sadly.
11. You drive very slow / slowly.

Comparisons

This jacket is small. Have you got anything bigger but as smart as this one?
This jacket is small too and it's more expensive than the others.
What?! You're the most horrible assistant I've ever met.
This is the biggest size we've got and it's very cheap.
And you're the rudest man I've ever met.

Comparison of Adjectives

Adjectives of:	Positive	Comparative	Superlative
one syllable	long	longer than	the longest of/in
two syllables ending in -y, -w, -er	happy	happier than	the happiest of/in
two or more syllables	modern beautiful	more modern than more beautiful than	the most modern of/in the most beautiful of/in

1. **We use the comparative to compare two people or things and the superlative to compare three or more people or things.**
   Jenny is **younger than** Mary. Jenny is **the youngest of** all her friends.

2. **We use than with the comparative and the ... of / in with the superlative. We use in with the superlative, usually when we refer to places.**
   London is **bigger than** Leeds. It is **the biggest** city **in** England.

3. **Some adjectives form their comparatives either by adding -er / -est or with more / most.**
   Some of these are : **clever, stupid, narrow, gentle.**
   clever - cleverer - the cleverest **OR** clever - more clever - the most clever

Spelling

Adjectives ending in :		
- e ➡ - r / - st	- y̸ ➡ - ier / - iest	one stressed vowel between two consonants - double the consonant
large - larger - largest	heavy - heavier - heaviest	big - bigger - biggest

177 Fill in the blanks with the correct comparative and superlative forms.

1. tall .. *taller*...... . *tallest* .....
2. careful ....
3. cheap ....
4. fat ....
5. interesting ....
6. modern ....
7. nice ....
8. fast ....
9. thin ....
10. popular ....

Comparison of Adverbs

	Positive	Comparative	Superlative
Adverbs with the same form as adjectives	hard	harder	the hardest
two-syllable adverbs	early	earlier	the earliest
compound adverbs (adjective + -ly) (slow - slowly)	slowly	more slowly	the most slowly

178 Fill in the blanks with the correct comparative and superlative forms.

1. cheaply *more cheaply* *most cheaply*
2. fast ....
3. quickly ....
4. early ....
5. late ....
6. loudly ....
7. hard ....
8. politely ....

Irregular Forms

Positive	Comparative	Superlative
good/well	better	best
bad/badly	worse	worst
much	more	most
many/a lot of	more	most
little	less	least
far	further/farther	furthest/farthest

further/farther = longer (in distance)
I can't run any further/farther.
further = more
There is no further news at the moment.

179 Fill in the table with the correct forms.

1. quick	.... *quicker*	.... *quickest* ....
2. boring	....	....
3.	better	....
4.	....	least
5. hard	....	....
6.	....	most
7.	worse	....
8. dangerous	....	....
9.	further	....
10.	cleverer/more clever	....
11. quietly	....	....
12. easy	....	....

180 Complete the sentences.

1. Mary is ....
... *thinner than* ..
Ann. (thin)

2. This bike is ....
....
this car. (cheap)

3. John is ....
....
all. (heavy)

4. Dolphins are ....
....
mammals of all after man. (intelligent)

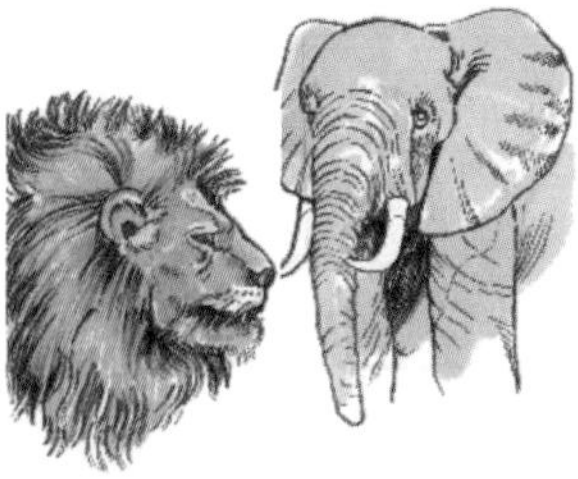

5. A lion is ....
....
an elephant. (dangerous)

6. Ben is ....
.... athlete
of all. (good)

181 Write sentences about places you know as in the example :

1. (beautiful) .... *The most beautiful place I know is Venice.* ....
2. (expensive) ....
3. (cheap) ....
4. (cold) ....
5. (hot) ....
6. (ancient) ....

182 Complete the sentences as in the example :

1. It rained .... *more heavily* .... yesterday .... *than* .... today. (heavily)
2. Ann talks .... Pam. (loud)
3. He earns .... money .... his brother. (much)
4. She is .... student .... the class. (hard-working)
5. This is .... film .... all. (exciting)
6. She runs .... me. (fast)
7. This exercise is .... that one. (difficult)
8. Onassis was one of .... men .... the world. (rich)

as ... as is used to compare two people or things which are the same. He's **as tall as** Peter.

not as / so ... as is used in negative sentences. He isn't **as / so rich as** John.

183 Write sentences as in the example :

1. (expensive)
The ring .. *is as* ...
.. *expensive as* ...
the watch.

2. (tall)
Peter ....
..........Ben.

Christine 72 Helen 74

3. (old)
Christine ....
....
.... Helen.

4. (poor)
Richard ....
....
Ted.

184 Complete the sentences with "in", "of", "than", "as ... as", or "the" .

There are six of us in our family: Mum, Dad, my two brothers, Peter and Tony, my sister Tina and me. My two brothers are older 1) ..... *than* .... me. Peter is 2) .... oldest but Tony is taller 3) .... him. Tony is two years younger 4) .... Peter, though. Tina is 5) .... tall .... I am but her hair is longer and she is heavier 6) .... me. I think she is more intelligent 7) .... me. My mother says I am 8) .... most helpful 9) .... all but my father says that I am 10) .... noisiest 11) .... all. I don't know if that is true - but we are 12) .... happiest family 13) .... the street.

185 Spot the differences between Frank and Gavin.

1. .... *Frank's fishing rod is longer than Gavin's.*.......................................
2. ....
3. ....
4. ....
5. ....
6. ....
7. ....
8. ....
9. ....
10. ....

186 Write comparisons as in the example :

1. (long/short)
Mary's hair ... *is* ....
.... *longer than* .....
Jean's. Jean's hair
.. *is shorter than* ..
Mary's. Jean's hair
isn't .. *as long as* ...
Mary's.

2. (many/few)
Kate has got ....
books .... Chris.
Chris has got ....
books ....Kate.
Chris hasn't got ....
....
books .... Kate.

3. (big/small)
A cat is ....
.... mouse.
A mouse is.............
.......................cat.
A mouse isn't..........
.... cat.

4. (much/little)
Robert has got ....
money ....Fiona.
Fiona has got..........
money ....Robert.
Fiona hasn't got.......
money ....Robert.

187 Use the following adjectives to write sentences comparing the three girls.

young, heavy, tall, a lot of, expensive

Joan

Age : 27
Height : 1.67 m
Weight : 70 kilos
Salary : £1,000
Car : £13,000

Anne

Age : 25
Height : 1.68 m
Weight : 72 kilos
Salary : £800
Car : £9,000

Margaret

Age : 23
Height : 1.70 m
Weight : 73 kilos
Salary : £950
Car : £12,000

.... *Joan, Anne and Margaret are teachers. Joan is young. Anne is younger* ....
.... *than Joan. She isn't as young as Margaret, though. Margaret is the youngest* ....
.... *of them all.*...
....
....
....
....
....
....
....

Now compare yourself with Margaret.

...... *I am younger than Margaret.* ....
....
....
....
....

188 Complete Jim's letter.

Dear Anna,

Here I am in Las Vegas! I'm having a wonderful time. The weather is 1) **hotter** (hot) and 2) .... (dry) in England. The houses are 3) .... (big) ours and the cars are 4) .... (long) and 5) .... (wide) those in our country. I love the food here. Yesterday I had 6) .... (good) hamburger I've ever eaten! The hotel is beautiful; I think it's 7) .... (beautiful) hotel I've ever seen. At the moment I am in a casino; it's 8) .... (big) in the world and it's 9) .... (busy) in town. I'll phone you when I get back.

Love, Jim

Oral Activity 25

The teacher divides the class into two teams and starts saying adjectives or adverbs. The teams in turn give the comparative forms of the adjective / adverb in question. Each correct response gets 1 point. The team with the most points is the winner.

Teacher:	big
Team A S1:	bigger - biggest
Teacher:	careful
Team B S1:	more careful - most careful
Teacher:	early
Team A S2:	more early - most early
Teacher:	Wrong! earlier - earliest.
	Team A doesn't get a point.

Oral Activity 26 (The Ideal Person)

The teacher divides the class into two teams. Each team decides on an imaginary ideal person to support and compare with the other team's ideal person. Team A, for example, supports "Beth" and Team B supports "Bob". The teacher writes some ideas on the board - **clever, quiet, helpful, good, happy, generous, healthy, clean, tidy, friendly, polite** etc. When a team makes a mistake or fails to give a sentence to support the ideal person, the team does not get a point.

Team A S1:	Beth is more helpful than Bob.
Team B S1:	Yes, but Bob is tidier than Beth.
Team A S2:	Beth is quieter than Bob.
Team B S2:	Yes, but Bob is cleanest than Beth.
Teacher:	No! Bob is cleaner than Beth. Team B doesn't get a point.

Writing Activity 14

Compare two people you know a lot about (your father and mother, a friend and yourself, two friends of yours or two famous singers).

15. Modal Verbs

The modal verbs are: can, could, must, need, will, would, shall etc. They have the same form in all persons. They come before the subject in questions and take "not" after them in negations. They take an infinitive without "to" after them.

Can she sing? No, she **can't** sing but she **can** dance.

Can - Could

Can is used to express ability in the present or to ask permission.	She **can** type. (ability in the present) **Can** I borrow your pen? (asking permission)
Could is used to express ability in the past, polite requests or to ask permission politely.	He **could** run fast when he was 17. (ability in the past) **Could** I have some tea? (polite request) **Could** I leave early, please? (asking permission)

189 Fill in "can", "can't", "could" or "couldn't".

When I was young I 1) .... *could* .... play sport but I 2) .... dance well. Now I'm old; I 3) .... climb the stairs, but I 4) .... sit in my armchair and watch TV.

190 **Spot the speech situations : ability in the present, ability in the past, asking permission, polite request or asking permission politely.**

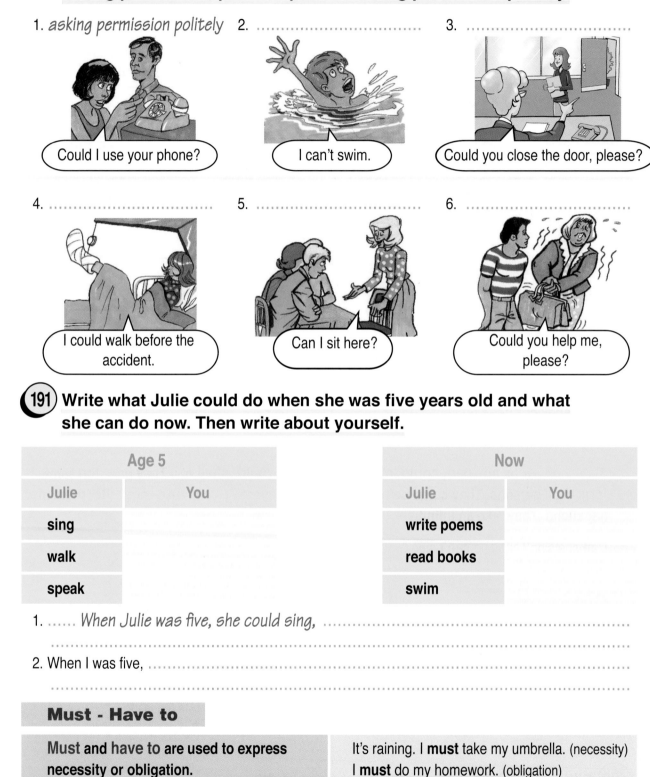

1. *asking permission politely*

Could I use your phone?

2. ....

I can't swim.

3. ....

Could you close the door, please?

4. ....

I could walk before the accident.

5. ....

Can I sit here?

6. ....

Could you help me, please?

191 **Write what Julie could do when she was five years old and what she can do now. Then write about yourself.**

Age 5	
Julie	You
sing	
walk	
speak	

Now	
Julie	You
write poems	
read books	
swim	

1. ...... *When Julie was five, she could sing,* ....

....

2. When I was five, ...

....

Must - Have to

Must and have to are used to express necessity or obligation.	It's raining. I **must** take my umbrella. (necessity) I **must** do my homework. (obligation) He **has to** go to hospital. (necessity)
"Have to" means that sb else decides. "Must" means that I decide.	Soldiers **have to** wear a uniform. I **must** work till late tonight.

192 Fill in "must" or "have to", then say who decides.

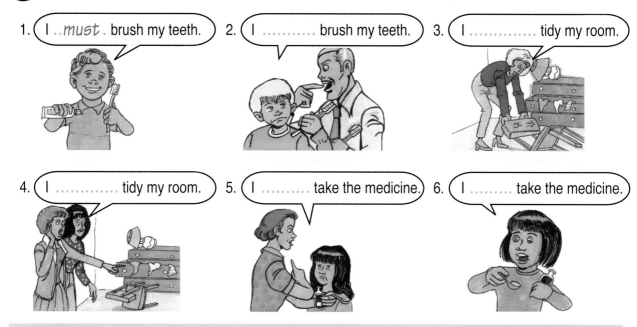

1. I *..must.* brush my teeth.

2. I .... brush my teeth.

3. I .... tidy my room.

4. I .... tidy my room.

5. I .... take the medicine.

6. I .... take the medicine.

"Must" is used only in the Present tense. It borrows the rest of its tenses from the verb "have to". "Have to" changes into "has to" in the third person singular in the present affirmative and into "had to" in all persons in the Past affirmative. Have to takes do / does / did to form its questions or negations and it is followed by a to - infinitive.
He **had to** leave early. **Did she have to** leave early, too?
She **doesn't have to** finish it now. She **has to** finish it by Monday.

193 Write what Ann "has to do" or "doesn't have to do" in the office. Then write about yourself.

Ann		You
sort out the morning post	✓	get up early at weekends
type letters	✗	visit my grandparents on Sundays
answer the phone	✓	do housework every day
clean the office	✗	help Mother wash up
fill in reports	✓	take exams this year
lock up the office	✗	study hard

.... *Ann has to sort out the morning post.* ....

....

....

....

....

194 Fill in "have to", "has to", "don't / doesn't have to", "didn't have to", "had to" or "won't have to".

1. It's Sunday tomorrow so I .... *won't have to* .... get up early.
2. There's no school tomorrow, so the children .... go to bed early.
3. We went to a restaurant yesterday, so we .... cook.
4. Let's clean up now, so we .... do it tomorrow.
5. It rained yesterday, so I .... water the flowers.
6. Lucy feels better now, so she .... take the medicine.
7. You've got plenty of time. You .... hurry.
8. He .... shout or else she can't hear him.
9. It was very cold yesterday so I .... wear a coat.
10. She .... wear glasses or else she can't read.
11. I can't go out tonight. I .... study for my exam.
12. I took the dog for a walk this morning so you .... take it out tonight.
13. My car doesn't work, so I .... take the train.
14. I broke my tooth, so I .... go to the dentist's yesterday.

Must - mustn't - needn't

Must	**expresses obligation or necessity.**	You **must** tell the truth.
Mustn't	**expresses prohibition.**	You **mustn't** drive fast.
Needn't	**expresses no necessity.**	There's enough bread. You **needn't** buy any.

195 Fill in "must", "mustn't" or "needn't" as in the example:

1. You ... *mustn't* ...... fight.

2. They .... wash the dishes.

3. You .... tell anyone. It's a secret.

4. Your shoes are dirty. You .... clean them.

5. You .... let the dog sleep in your bed.

6. You .... feed the cat. It isn't hungry.

7. They .... go out today. They .... stay in bed.

8. We .... buy any eggs. We have a lot.

9. You .... feed the animals at the zoo.

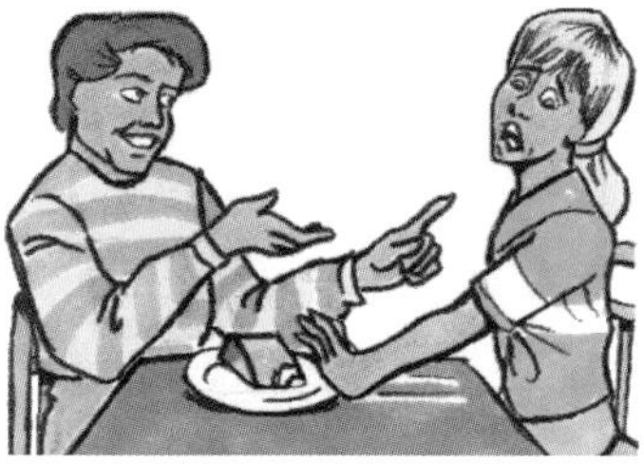

10. You .... eat it if you don't like it.

11. She .... be late for work.

12. You .... tidy your room.

196 Fill in the gaps with "mustn't" or "needn't".

A teacher is speaking to his students before a test:

"You are going to have a test today. Your test papers are on your desks. You 1) ...... *mustn't* .... begin until I tell you. You 2) .... hurry; you have plenty of time. You 3) .... speak during the test. You 4) .... copy your friends' work and you 5) .... open any of your books. You 6) .... write in pen; if you prefer you can write in pencil. You 7) .... stay when you've finished; you can leave if you want to, but you 8) .... be noisy. When you leave you 9) .... wait for your friends outside the classroom. Wait outside the building! Finally, I wish you all good luck. You can begin now!"

Shall - Will - Would

Shall	**is used with "I" or "We" in questions, suggestions or offers.** **Shall we** go to the cinema tonight?
Will	**is used to express predictions, warnings, offers, promises, threats, requests, suggestions, on-the-spot decisions, opinions, hopes and fears.** Try harder or **you'll** fail your exams.
Would	**is used to express polite or formal requests.** **Would you** carry my suitcase?
Would like	**is used to express polite or formal offers and suggestions.** **Would you like** to come with me to the party?

197 Match the pictures with the sentences, then spot the speech situations.

Will you post this letter, please?
Would you type these letters, please?
Shall I close the window?
It's raining. I'll put up my umbrella.
Would you like to drink some wine?
Shall we go by taxi?
Would you like me to answer the phone?
You will get fat if you eat so much.
I hope she will come on time.

hope, (polite) request, warning, suggestion, offer, on-the-spot decision

1. ...... *hope* ....

.. *I hope she will come*...
..... *on time*...............

2. ....

....
....

3. ....

....
....

4. ....

....
....

5. ....

....
....

6. ....

....
....

7. ....

....
....

8. ....

....
....

9. ....

....
....

198 Fill in "could", "shall", "mustn't", "can", "needn't" or "will".

We 1) ... *needn't* ...... study tomorrow as it's Saturday, so 2) .... we go to the beach? We 3) .... .take some sandwiches to eat; 4) .... you bring something to drink? 5) .... you invite your sister too? We 6) .... be late home though, as I'm going out at 7 o'clock.

199 Fill in the correct modal verb.

1. I don't feel well, ... *could/can/would* .... you call a doctor?
2. .... I help you move the furniture?
3. .... you iron the clothes, please?
4. .... we go climbing? No, let's go swimming.
5. You .... shout, I can hear you.
6. You .... come to the party if you don't want to.
7. You .... brush your teeth after meals.
8. "I'm hungry". "Don't worry – I .... make a sandwich for you".
9. Where .... we go on holiday this year?
10. A fish .... swim but it .... fly.
11. She is very rich. She .... work.
12. He .... read when he was seven but he .... not swim.
13. You .... be late for dinner tonight. We're having guests.
14. He's got a cold. He .... stay in bed for a week.
15. I haven't got any money. .... you lend me some?

Oral Activity 27

The teacher divides the class into two teams. Then he/she says a modal verb. The teams make up sentences in turn. Each correct sentence gets 1 point. If one team fails to give a correct sentence, it doesn't get a point.

Teacher:	mustn't
Team A S1:	You mustn't tell lies.
Teacher:	shall
Team B S1:	Shall they come tonight?
Teacher:	Wrong! Team B doesn't get a point.

Oral Activity 28

The teacher writes some cues on the board: **a pen, a book, some milk, a cake, a bicycle, a car, a ball, some water, a hat, a record, a chair, a toothbrush, a flower, an ice-cream** etc. Then play the game in two teams as follows:

Teacher:	You've got a book. What can you do with it?
Team A S1:	I can read it. (Team A gets a point.)
Teacher:	You've got a pen. What can you do with it?
Team B S1:	I can .... (S1 fails to answer)
Teacher:	Team B doesn't get a point.

Writing Activity 15

Write six things you must do or you mustn't do today. e.g. I must do my homework. etc.

16. Infinitive — The "-ing form" / Too - Enough

You're too serious. You must be more cheerful with the customers, George!
Good morning sir! I hate doing this but am I funny enough now?
No, George, you're too funny! Stop doing that!
But sir, you told me to be cheerful with the customers.

Infinitive — The "-ing form"	
1. We use "to-infinitive" to express purpose. Why did you go to the baker's? **To buy** bread.	**1. We use the "-ing form" as a noun.** I like **swimming**.
2. We use "to-infinitive" after "want" and "would love/like". I would like **to visit** Madrid.	**2. We use the "-ing form" after the verbs : enjoy, love, hate, like, dislike, stop.** He enjoys **reading**.
3. We use infinitive without to after the modal verbs (can, must, will etc). He can **dance** but he can't **sing**.	**3. We use the "-ing form" after "go" for physical activities.** He goes **fishing** every Sunday.

200 **Write what these people like doing and what they want to be.**

1. Tina ... *likes singing. She* .. *wants to be a singer*..

2. Ben ....
....

3. Bob and Sally ....
....

4. Tom ....
....

5. Mary ....
....

6. They ....
....

Too - Enough	
Too + adjective / adverb means more than is wanted. The implication is always negative.	He's **too young** to travel alone. (He can't travel alone.) He drove **too slowly** to win the race. (He didn't drive fast enough to win the race.)
Adjective / adverb + enough means as much as is wanted.	She's **old enough** to drive a car. (She can drive a car.) He left **early enough** to catch the train. (He left early so he was able to catch the train.)
Enough + noun	He's got **enough money** to buy a car.

201 Complete the sentences with "too" or "enough" and one of the adjectives from the list below:

big, short, long, heavy, cheap , light, tall

1. Sally can't wear that skirt.
It's .... *too short.* ....

2. Tony won't buy those shoes.
They aren't ....

3. Ann can't wear that coat.
It's ....

4. Peter won't buy those jeans. They are ....

5. Chris can't buy this watch.
It isn't ....

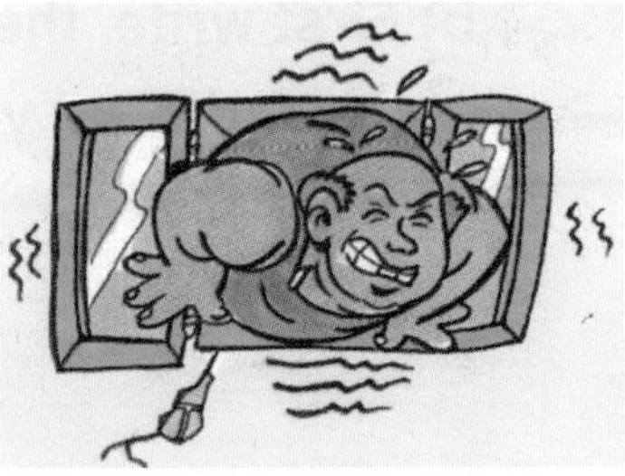

6. Ted can't get through the window. He is ....

7. She can carry the suitcase.
It's ....

8. He can't carry the suitcase.
It's ....

9. John can reach the cake.
He is ....

202 **a) Write where these people want to go and what they would like to see there.**

	Paris / The Eiffel Tower	London / Big Ben	Egypt / The Pyramids	Athens / The Acropolis
Alison	✓			
Niki				✓
Chris & Ann			✓	
Richard		✓		
You				

1. Alison ...... *wants to go to Paris. She would like to see the Eiffel Tower.* ....
2. Niki ....
3. Chris & Ann ....
4. Richard ....
5. I ....

b) First write, then tell your teacher/friend about six places you want to go to and what you would like to see there.

....
....
....
....
....
....

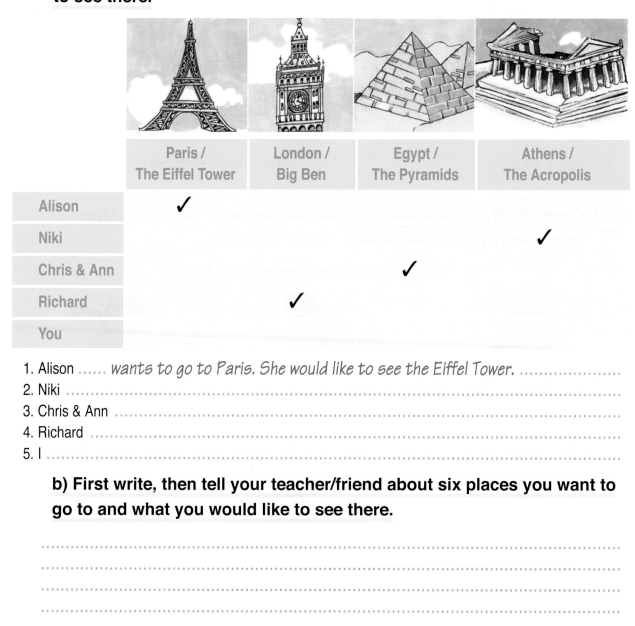

203 Write what these people like or don't like doing, then write about yourself.

	watch TV	dance	eat out	sing	cook	paint
Albert	✓		✓	✓		✓
Ann		✓	✓	✓	✓	
Jenny & Peter	✓			✓	✓	✓
You						

1. Albert .... *likes watching TV. He also likes eating out, singing and painting, but he* .... *doesn't like dancing or cooking.* ....
2. Ann ....
3. Jenny and Peter ....
4. I ....

204 Put the verbs in brackets into the "to-infinitive form" or the "-ing form".

Paul: I want 1) .... *to go* .... (go) to the cinema tonight. The new James Bond film is on. Would you like 2) .... (come) with me?

Simon: I don't like 3) .... (go) to the cinema but if you want 4) .... (go), then I'll come with you.

Ann: I like 5) .... (go) to discos and I enjoy 6) .... (ski). What do you like 7) .... (do)?

Sam: I like 8) .... (windsurf). I often go 9) .... (climb), too. I hate 10) .... (cycle), though.

Ann: Why did you go 11) .... (cycle) yesterday then?

Sam: I wanted 12) .... (avoid) Peter. I didn't want 13) .... (go) out with him.

205 Put the verbs in brackets into the infinitive form (with or without "to").

A: Shall we 1) .... *go* .... (go) out tonight?

B: I can't. I have 2) .... (go) to my aunt's. I must 3) .... (say) goodbye to my cousin. He's leaving tomorrow.

A: Will you 4) .... (be) late?

B: I don't know. I would like 5) .... (go) out with you, though. Can I 6) .... (call) you later and let you know?

A: Yes, sure. I'll 7) .... (be) in the office until 7 o'clock. I want 8) .... (finish) some letters.

206 Answer the questions using "too" or "enough".

1. Can he go into the pub?
No, he can't. (old)
He isn't ... *old enough.* ...

2. Can he pay for his dinner?
No, he can't. (money)
He hasn't got ....

3. Can he lift the table?
Yes, he can. (strong)
He is ....

4. Can Sally go to the party?
No, she can't. (ill)
She is ....

5. Can he climb the tree?
No, he can't. (old)
He is ....

6. Can she wear the dress?
Yes, she can. (big)
It is ....

7. Can he buy the bicycle?
Yes, he can. (money)
He's got........................

8. Can he buy her dinner?
No, he can't. (poor)
He is ....

9. Can she drink the tea?
No, she can't. (hot)
It's ....

Oral Activity 29

The teacher divides the class into two teams and chooses a leader. He/she gives the leader a list of objects. The leader asks the teams questions and the teams answer in turn. Each correct answer gets 1 point. The team with the most points is the winner.

Leader's list: **pen, cup, book, paper, eggs, tomatoes, sandwich**

Leader:	Why do you want a pen?
Team A S1:	To write a letter.
Leader:	Why do you want a cup?
Team B S1:	To drink tea.

Leader:	Why do you want a book?
Team A S2:	To wear.
Leader:	Wrong! To read. Team A doesn't get a point.

Oral Activity 30

The teacher asks students to say what they like doing and don't like doing.

S1: I like swimming but I don't like sunbathing.
S2: I like dancing but I don't like singing. etc.

Writing Activity 16

Write down three things you like doing and another three things you hate doing.

Revision Exercises IV

207 Find the mistake.

1. The policeman arrested the ~~thiefs~~. .... *thieves* ....
2. Be careful! You'll have an accident. ....
3. "What are you?" "Tom Smith." ....
4. You like pizza? ....
5. I want being a teacher. ....
6. John went to ski yesterday. ....
7. I hope I'm going to pass the test. ....
8. They play in the garden now. ....
9. Mother is standing in the window. ....
10. We went there on car. ....
11. He swims fastest than me. ....
12. They got married in December 27th. ....
13. She didn't finish her work yet. ....
14. There isn't someone in the room. ....
15. We must wear uniforms at work. ....
16. She's the taller of all. ....
17. You needn't be rude to your parents. ....
18. Do she play the violin? ....
19. Ann is lieing on the grass. ....
20. He usually watch TV in the evenings. ....
21. Sam did good in the test. ....

208 Choose the correct item.

1. He always .... *C*.............. at 7 o'clock.
   A) is getting up B) has got up C) gets up
2. Ann .... to Paris in 1991.
   A) has moved B) moved C) moves

3. We haven't heard from him .... months.
   A) since B) yet C) for

4. He goes to work .... taxi.
   A) on B) by C) in

5. .... we go out tonight?
   A) Shall B) Will C) Have

6. You ...... cross the street without looking first.
   A) mustn't B) don't have to C) needn't

7. He's wearing .... uniform.
   A) —- B) an C) a

8. Mark is as .... as Greg.
   A) taller B) tall C) tallest

9. He .... his car a month ago.
   A) bought B) buys C) has bought

10. Claire dances .... than Sue.
    A) better B) well C) best

11. .... is Ted? In his bedroom.
    A) Where B) What C) Who

12. Peter is the .... student in the class.
    A) better B) good C) best

13. .... you lend me £10, please?
    A) Shall B) Could C) Must

14. Look at him! He .... across the street.
    A) is running B) runs C) ran

15. This is .... umbrella.
    A) Mary B) Mary's C) Marys'

16. There aren't .... flowers in the vase.
    A) some B) no C) any

17. .... left first? Peter.
    A) What B) Who C) Which

18. I haven't got .... bread.
    A) many B) much C) lot of

19. He .... to work since Monday.
    A) won't come B) didn't come C) hasn't come

20. I promise I .... you a new sweater.
    A) am going to buy B) bought C) will buy

209 Look at the pictures and ask subject and object questions.

Tony gave Ann a present. Ann lent Jane some money. Jane gave the money to Kevin. Kevin bought some flowers for Tina. Tina gave a letter to George.

Tony Ann Jane Kevin Tina George

1. .... *Who gave Ann a present?* .... Tony.
2. .... A present.
3. .... To Ann.
4. .... Ann.
5. .... Some flowers.
6. .... To Kevin.
7. .... A letter.
8. .... Tina.
9. .... Jane.
10. .... To George.
11. .... For Tina.
12. .... To nobody.

210 Complete the conversation between Mr Muggins and the shopkeeper using "any", "a lot", "many", "a little", "a few" or "much".

Mr Muggins: Good morning!
Shopkeeper: Good morning, Mrs Muggins. Do you need 1) .... *many* .... things today?
Mr Muggins: No, not 2) .... Have you got 3) .... coffee?
Shopkeeper: We only have 4) .... jars.
Mr Muggins: I'll take one, please. I'd like 5) .... butter, please.
Shopkeeper: How 6) ....?
Mr Muggins: A kilo.
Shopkeeper: Oh no! I'm sorry, there isn't that 7) .... left! But we do have 8) .... margarine.
Mr Muggins: That's okay. I want some oranges, too. But I don't want 9) .... , only 10) ....
Shopkeeper: How 11) .... ?
Mr Muggins: Four, please.
Shopkeeper: Here you are.
Mr Muggins: Do you have 12) .... strawberries?
Shopkeeper: No, but we have 13) .... blackberries.
Mr Muggins: No, thank you. That's all. How 14) .... money do you want?
Shopkeeper: £2.50.
Mr Muggins: £2.50!! That's 15) ....! I'm not coming here again. Goodbye!

211 Fill in the correct tense of the verbs in brackets.

Madonna 1) .... *is* .. (be) a famous singer. She 2) .... (act) in several films as well. She 3) .... (write) a book some time ago which 4) .... (become) very popular. She 5) .... (be) married to Sean Penn who 6) .... (be) an American actor, but they 7) .... (get divorced) a few years ago. Madonna 8) .... (not/have) any children yet, but she 9) .... (say) she 10) .... (have) children in the future. She 11) .... (travel) all over the world giving concerts. She 12) .... (have) many hit songs already and she 13) .... (make) more records in the future. She 14) .... (act) in more films too. She 15) .... (become) famous in the 1980's and she 16) .... (be) now a millionairess.

212 A. Fill in "something", "anything" or "nothing".

Judy: Do you know 1) .... *anything* .... about the Michael Jackson concert?
Bobby: No, 2) .... Sorry. Perhaps Tina knows 3) ....
Judy: No, she doesn't know 4) .... about it either.

Bobby: Well, ask John. I'm sure he will know 5) .... about it.

B. Fill in "somebody", "anybody" or "nobody".

Judy: John, 1) ...... *nobody* .... knows anything about the Michael Jackson concert! Do you?
John: Of course. He's so famous, I thought everybody would know about it!
Judy: Do you know 2) .... who has got tickets for it?
John: There was 3) .... selling tickets outside the record shop yesterday. Perhaps they are there again today.

C. Fill in "somewhere", "anywhere" or "nowhere".

Judy: I've looked everywhere in town today. I could find tickets for the concert 1) ...... *nowhere* ...... There weren't any left 2) ....
John: Wait a minute! I'm sure I saw some tickets 3) .... this morning. Yes! I remember! Here are two tickets. One for you and one for me. We'll go together!!

213 Put the verbs into the "Present Simple", "Present Perfect", "Past Simple" or "Future".

My name 1) .... *is* .... (be) Julie Baker. I 2) .... (be) twenty-five years old. I'm from America but I 3) .... (live) in London since 1985. I 4) .... (work) in a bank since then. I 5) .... (never/be) married and I 6) .... (not/have) any children. I 7) .... (enjoy) reading, going to the theatre and meeting interesting people. I 8) .... (be) a friendly person and I 9) .... (have) a good sense of humour. I 10) .... (never/smoke) a cigarette in my life. I 11) .... (join) ASH in 1984 and since then I 12) .... (take) part in campaigns against smoking. 13) .... (you/join) us?

214 Fill in "in", "at" or "on".

1. I always go into town ..... *on* .... Saturday.
2. We get up .... 7.30.
3. We'll go there .... the morning.
4. They give each other presents .... Christmas.
5. She went to the theatre .... her birthday.
6. St Valentine's Day is .... February.
7. You must come here .... Friday morning.
8. I finish work .... 5.30 p.m.
9. We go to church .... Easter.
10. The party is .... Monday.
11. My father works .... night.
12. .... summer we go to the beach.
13. Phone me .... nine o'clock.
14. He will leave school .... June.

215 Put the verbs in brackets into the "Present Simple" or "Present Continuous".

Dear Mother,

How 1) .... *are* ... (be) you? I 2) .... (sit) in a café near my house. I 3) .... (like) my work, but it 4) .... (be) difficult sometimes. Today, David 5) .... (mend) his boat. Every Saturday he 6) .... (work) on it. I 7) .... (drink) a cup of coffee and I 8) .... (think) of your coffee at home! Every day I 9) .... (drive) to work. It 10) .... (take) me half an hour. 11) .... (Dad/still/work) at the office? During the week David 12) .... (work) in a shop in the centre. He 13) .... (travel) a lot by car too. The sun 14) .... (shine) at the moment, and the weather 15) .... (be) beautiful for autumn. 16) .... (you/enjoy) your new job? Well, I must go now. David 17) .... (come) across the road. Write soon.

Love,
Maria

216 Complete this dialogue.

A: Good morning, madam. 1) *Can I help you* ...?
B: Yes, please. I'm looking for a dress.
A: 2) .... ?
B: I want a red one.
A: 3) .... ?
B: I'm size 12.
A: I've got one here. 4) .... ?
B: Yes, a lot. Can I try it on?
A: Of course. There's a changing room here. Well, 5) .... ?
B: It's nice. It fits me beautifully. 6) .... ?
A: £45.
B: I'll take it.

217 Ask questions to which the highlighted words are the answers.

1. Mary saw Chris. .... *Who saw Chris?* ....
2. Mary saw Chris. ....
3. Lucy will write to Jean. ....
4. Lucy will write to Jean. ....
5. Paul works with Peter. ....
6. Paul works with Peter. ....
7. Sally met Nicholas. ....
8. Sally met Nicholas. ....
9. Paul has invited Christine. ....
10. Paul has invited Christine. ....

218 Compare picture A to picture B as in the example :

Picture A

Picture B

1. .... *The doll is taller. It has got longer hair. Its dress is shorter.* ....
2. ....
3. ....
4. ....
5. ....
6. ....

219 Jane's mother is going to work. She is telling Jane what she wants her to do. Fill in "must", "have to", "mustn't" or "needn't".

Mother: Jane, you 1) .... *must* .... tidy your room while I'm out.
Jane: But Mum, I want to watch TV.
Mother: You can watch TV later.
Jane: 2) .... I .... wash the windows, too?
Mother: No, you 3) .... wash the windows and you 4) .... polish the furniture either.
Jane: Do you want me to clean the kitchen as well?
Mother: No, there are a lot of switches in there. You 5)..................... touch them.
Jane: Okay, Mum. Will you bring me some chocolates?
Mother: I will, but you 6) .... eat them all at once or you'll be sick.

220 Fill in "the" where necessary.

1) ..X... Nicole comes from 2) .... Paris but she lives in 3) .... Manchester. 4) .... her neighbours, 5) .... Browns, are from 6) .... Leeds. 7) .... people who live on 8) .... other side are from 9) .... Liverpool. They work in 10) .... factory opposite 11) .... Nicole's house.

221 A doctor is talking to his patient. Fill in "must", "mustn't" or "needn't".

You are much better Mr Brown and you 1) *needn't* stay in hospital any longer. You can go home today. However, you 2) .... go back to work for two weeks. You 3) .... stay in bed all day but you 4) .... go outside for a week. You 5) .... smoke any cigarettes and you 6) .... drink alcohol. You 7) .... remember to take your medicine every four hours. You 8) .... get very tired so you 9) .... have any visitors if you don't want to. Finally, you 10) .... leave today until the nurse gives you all your medicine.

222 Put the verbs in brackets into the "to-infinitive form" or the "-ing form".

John and his family love 1) .... *going* ... (go) to the zoo. They enjoy 2) .... (watch) the monkeys. John's mother hates 3) .... (see) the crocodiles. She doesn't want 4) .... (go) near them. John and his sister like 5) .... (watch) the lions. When John grows up, he wants 6) .... (be) a lion-tamer. John's father likes 7) ....(listen) to the exotic birds and 8) .... (see) them fly. He would like 9) .... (have) one at home but he can't because these birds can't live in houses. Sometimes he goes 10)................ .... (birdwatch) and takes photographs of the birds he sees.

223 Fill in "a", "an" or "the".

Mum : There are too many things lying on 1) ... *the* ... table. There's 2) .... book, 3) .... newspaper, 4) .... magazine and 5) .... address book.

Sally : Ok, Mum. I'll put 6) .... newspaper, 7) .... magazine and 8) .... book in 9) .... magazine rack and I'll take10) .... address book and put it by 11) .... phone in 12) .... hall.

Mum : Thanks, and don't leave them lying around again!

224 Complete the dialogue as in the example :

A: 1) .... *Where did you go last night?*............
B: I went to the fast-food restaurant.
A: 2) .... with you?
B: John and Helen.
A: 3) .... ?
B: Cheeseburgers and chips.
A: 4) .... ?
B: We left at 9:30.
A: 5) .... so early?
B: Because John had a headache.
A: Oh really? 6) .... now?
B: Much better. Well, 7) .... is your sister?
A: She is at home. She wants to study for a test.

225 Complete the dialogue as in the example:

Manager: Good morning, Miss Clark. Please sit down.
Now 1) .... *why do you want to work here?*.......
Miss Clark: I think it would be good experience for me.
Manager: 2) .... before?
Miss Clark: I worked for Grabbett and Son.
Manager: 3) .... ?
Miss Clark: Yes, I enjoyed it very much.
Manager: Then 4) .... ?
Miss Clark: I left because I wanted to work abroad.
Manager: I see. And 5) .... ?
Miss Clark: I only returned from Canada two weeks ago.
Manager: Well, thank you Miss Clark. 6) .... ?
Miss Clark: Yes, I have some questions. 7) .... ?
Manager: It's £10,000 a year.
Miss Clark: And 8) .... ?
Manager: Seven hours a day. Well, Miss Clark, when will you be able to start?

226 Put the verbs in brackets into the correct tense.

Boys and girls, please remember that next week is the school trip. Students who 1) *are studying* (study) Art 2) .... (go) to the museum and History students 3) .... (visit) Stratford-upon-Avon. Shakespeare 4) .... (live) there and that's where he 5) .... (write) "The Tempest" . Stratford-upon-Avon 6) .... (be) one hundred miles away, so we 7) .... (leave) very early in the morning.

227 Fill in "my", "her", "his", "your", "our", "their" or "its".

Dear Jane,

Hello, 1) .. *my* .. name is Helen and I am from England. I would like to be 2) .... penfriend. I have got a sister. 3) .... name is Patty. She is married and 4) .... husband's name is Mark. They have got a pet dog; 5) .... name is Scamp. My father is a teacher. 6) .... name is Peter. My mother is a doctor. 7) .... name is Pamela. Do you have any brothers or sisters? Please tell me 8) .... names in 9) .... letter. In 10) .... next letter I will send you a photo of 11) .... family and 12) .... house. It is a big house and 13) .... garden is lovely too. Please write soon.

Love,
Helen

228 Fill in "since", "for", "ago", "yet" or "already".

1. We went to Paris three weeks ..... *ago* ....
2. I haven't seen him ....
3. I have .... met them.
4. She's been at work .... 8.00 a.m.
5. He left work three hours ....
6. They have lived there .... 2 years.
7. I've been in Germany .... a long time.
8. We have .... finished lunch.
9. We haven't found a new house ....
10. You haven't telephoned him .... last week.
11. She has .... done the washing-up.

229 Put the verbs in brackets into the "Present Simple", "Present Continuous", "Past Simple" or "Future Simple".

Mr Smith: Peter, I 1) .... *need* .... (need) this letter. Can you type it for me, please?
Peter: Yes, of course. Who 2) .... (be) the letter for?
Mr Smith: I 3) .... (write) to the bank again about the loan I 4) .... (ask) them about last month.
Peter: Oh yes, I 5) .... (remember); but Mrs Carr 6) .... (need) a letter, too. I 7) .... (type) it now. As soon as I finish it, I 8) .... (start) your letter. When it is ready, I 9) .... (bring) it to your office.
Mr Smith: Thank you. I 10) .... (want) it by noon.
Peter: Okay Mr Smith. It 11) .... (be) ready by then.

230 A famous painting has been stolen from the art gallery. The police are questioning Mr Laton, who works in the gallery. Read the dialogue and put the verbs in brackets into the "Present Simple", "Past Simple", "Future Simple" or "Present Perfect".

Policeman : Mr Laton, when 1) ...... *did you discover* .... (you / discover) the painting was missing?

Mr Laton : When I 2) .... (arrive) here at 8 o'clock in the morning. It 3) .... (be) there when I 4) .... (leave) last night at 9 o'clock. I 5) .... (think) someone 6) .... (steal) it during the night.

Policeman : How long 7) .... (you / be) at this gallery Mr Laton?

Mr Laton : I 8) .... (be) here for two months.

Policeman : What 9) .... (you / do) last night?

Mr Laton : I 10) .... (go) to the Rex cinema with my wife. We 11) .... (go) there every Thursday night.

Policeman : That 12) .... (be) very strange Mr Laton. That cinema 13) .... (be) closed last night.

Mr Laton : Oh yes, I 14) .... (make) a mistake. It (15) .... (be) Tuesday night. Last night. I ... umm umm ...

Policeman : I 16) .... (think) you 17) .... (have to) come to the police station with me, Mr Laton!

231 Put the adjectives or adverbs in brackets into the comparative forms.

In last year's Olympics the Russians were 1) ...... *better* .... (good) than all the other countries. The Americans won 2) .... (many) silver medals than the British but not as 3) .... (many) gold medals as the Russians. The Americans ran 4) .... (fast) than the British, but they did not jump as 5) .... (high) as the French. The Italians cycled the 6) .... (quickly) of all, but they were the 7) .... (slow) swimmers.

232 Change the sentences as in the example :

1. He's a fantastic cook. He cooks ...... *fantastically*.............
2. She's a careful driver. She drives....................................
3. He's a wonderful painter. He paints ....
4. She plays tennis well. She is a .... tennis player.
5. He runs quickly. He is a .... runner.

233 Fill in "on", "at" or "in".

This year I spent my summer holiday in Capri, Italy. I arrived there 1) . *on* .. August 1st, and stayed in my friends' villa for two weeks. 2) ...... the mornings we went swimming and water-skiing, 3) .... noon we had lunch and 4) ...... the evenings we went to a disco. I left 5) .... Monday morning but I promised to go back next year.

234 Fill in the blanks with "will" or "be going to" and the verb in brackets.

Dear Judy,

Thanks for your letter. I'm fine and so are my parents. Actually they 1) .. *are going to visit* .... (visit) my aunt next weekend so I 2) .... be) alone. If you can, 3) .... (you / come) and stay with me? I think we 4) .... (have) a great time. My sister 5) .... (have) a baby in June so my mother 6) .... (stay) with her for a while in London. I think it 7) .... (be) a girl. Can you believe it? I 8) .... (be) an auntie! Well, I must sign off because I have to leave or I 9) .... (miss) the bus. Call me to tell me if you can come.

Love, Paula

235 Fill in the blanks as in the example:

Australia and England are very different. Australia is much 1) .. *bigger* .. (big) 2) .. *than* .. England. It is much 3) .... (hot) and 4) .... (dry) 5) .... England and it has some of 6) .... (strange) animals 7) .... the world. England is 8) .... (green) 9) .... Australia because it is 10) .... (wet). It is 11) .... (small) but it has a 12) .... (big) population 13) .... Australia.The weather is 14) .... (cold) and it has a 15) .... (long) winter 16)..................... Australia but most English people believe it's 17) .... (good) country 18) .... the world. Do you agree?

236 Fill in "in", "on", "in front of", "round", "next to", "above","beside", "into" or "by".

Ann is 1) ..... *in* .... bed 2) .... hospital. 3) .... the bed there's a small table and 4) .... the table there's a vase of flowers. 5) .... the vase there's a glass of water. There's a TV set 6) .... the bed. 7) .... the bed there's a lovely picture. A nurse is standing 8) .... the bed. He's taking Ann's temperature. A doctor is coming 9) .... the room. She's holding some papers 10) .... her hands. There's a stethoscope 11) .... her neck.

Pre-Test 1 (Units 1-4)

A Fill in the blanks and answer the questions.

1 Look at ....!
.... a policeman?
....
.... a doctor.

2 Look at ....!
.... a dog?
....
.... a lion.

3 Look at ....!
.... teachers?
....
.... dancers.

B Fill in the blanks and answer the questions.

4 Look at ....!
.... a nurse?
....
.... a business woman.

5 Look at ....!
.... a horse?
....
.... a dog.

6 Look at ....!
.... policemen?
....
.... waiters.

C Fill in the plural.

7 one orange – two ....
8 one pencil – two ....
9 some soap – two ....
10 some honey – two ....
11 one peach – two ....
12 some bread – two ....
13 one goose – two ....
14 one cherry – two ....
15 some milk – two ....

D Fill in the plural.

16 one church – two ....
17 one fly – two ....
18 some chocolate – two ....
19 one mouse – two ....
20 one melon – two ....
21 one fox – two ....
22 some meat – two ....
23 one brush – two ....
24 some cheese – two ....

E Fill in she, they, its, their, her or his.

Mary is in the garden. **25)** .... is playing with **26)** .... brother. **27)** .... name is Ben. **28)** .... are both very happy. **29)** .... are playing with **30)** .... new dog; **31)** .... name is Sam.

F Fill in he, they, its, their, her or his.

This is my brother Tom. **32)** .... is twenty-three years old and **33)** .... hobbies are swimming and skiing. Tom also likes animals and **34)** .... has got two pets; a dog and a cat. **35)** .... names are Rumbo and Gretta. He has a fast bicycle and he likes riding it. **36)** .... colour is red! Laura, Tom's girlfriend, is twenty years old and it's **37)** .... birthday next week. **38)** .... are going to have dinner together in an expensive restaurant.

G Choose the correct item.

39 Look at the **womens'/women's** hats.
40 My **brother's/brothers** house is big.
41 This is **Robert's/Roberts'** book.
42 Look at the **houses windows/windows of the house**.
43 These are the **children's/childrens'** toys.
44 Look at the **chair's legs/legs of the chair**.

H Choose the correct item.

45 My **teacher's/teachers'** name is Mr Brown.
46 The **house's roof/roof of the house** is red.
47 Her **cousin's/cousins'** names are Betty and Kristi.
48 The **men's/mens'** ties are new.
49 Look at the **lady's/ladies'** dress.
50 This is the **food of the dog/dog's food**.

I Fill in a, an or some.

51	.... tea	**53**	.... umbrella	**55**	.... orange
52	.... banana	**54**	.... milk	**56**	.... bread

J Fill in a, an or some.

57	.... piano	**59**	.... pepper	**61**	.... furniture
58	.... money	**60**	.... egg	**62**	.... horse

K Choose the correct item.

63 That's .... book.
A mine B my C me

64 Paul is .... brother.
A Jenny B Jenny's C Jennys'

65 .... trees look lovely.
A The B A C This

66 Can I have a .... of water, please?
A bar B piece C glass

67 The .... are in the garden.
A child's B children C children's

68 There is .... wine in the bottle.
A a B some C the

69 Those sweets are ....
A my B me C mine

70 He lives in .... Paris.
A – B the C a

71 There are some .... in the park.
A people's B people C peoples'

72 Mum needs two .... of soap.
A bars B items C loaves

73 Look at ....!
A they B their C them

74 There are some .... on the farm.
A sheeps B sheep C sheep's

75 This is .... teacher.
A we B our C ours

76 These are .... grapes.
A Bill's B Bill C Bills'

77 There's .... sugar in the bowl.
A a B an C some

78 .... Eiffel Tower is in Paris.
A – B The C An

79 My uncle is .... teacher.
A the B a C some

80 Mary is .... sister.
A them B theirs C their

L Fill in have got, has got, is, are, am or can.

Martin and I **81)** .... friends. We **82)** .... computers. Martin's computer **83)** .... better than mine. He **84)** .... play more games on his computer. But I **85)** .... not unhappy because he **86)** .... a better computer.

M Fill in have got, has got, is, are, am or can.

I **87)** .... a pen friend. Her name **88)** .... Lucy and she **89)** .... a big sports car. She **90)** .... drive very fast. We **91)** .... the same age but I **92)** .... the one who is taller.

N Fill in this, that, these or those.

93 .... is a frog. 

94 .... are dogs.

95 .... is a man.

96 .... are books.

O Fill in this, that, these or those.

97 .... is a butterfly.

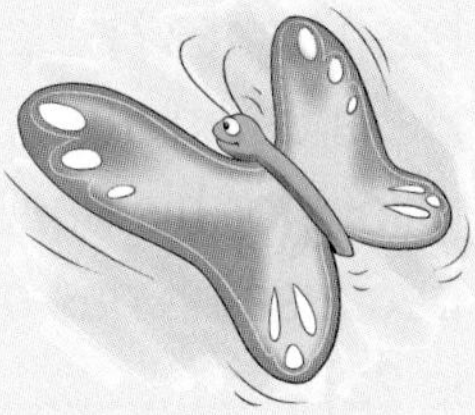

98 .... is a bicycle.

99 .... are birds.

100 .... are pencils.

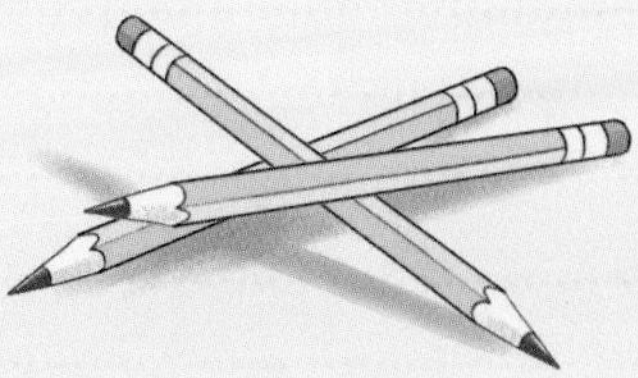

Pre-Test 2 (Units 1-8)

A Fill in much, many, (a) little or (a) few.

Billy needs to buy a lot of things but he hasn't got **1)** .... money. He has enough money to buy **2)** .... bread, **3)** .... cheese and **4)** .... eggs. There isn't **5)** .... milk left in the fridge and there is very **6)** .... tea. Luckily, there are still **7)** .... tins of food in the cupboard, but not **8)** ....

B Fill in much, many, (a) little or (a) few.

I like this café. It is very small so there is very **9)** .... room. There aren't **10)** .... chairs and there are very **11)** .... tables. I don't know **12)** .... of the people who come here, I only know **13)** .... of them. I come here **14)** .... times a week because I have **15)** .... free time.

C Fill in some, any, no or their derivatives.

There is **16)** .... sleeping on the bench. He hasn't got **17)** .... blankets to keep him warm. He is using **18)** .... newspapers. He has **19)** .... pillow for his head. He has **20)** .... to go because he has got **21)** .... friends. There is **22)** .... else in the park.

D Fill in some, any, no or their derivatives.

23) .... is sitting at the train station, waiting for a train. The café is closed, so she can't get **24)** .... to drink. There is **25)** .... to do and **26)** .... to talk to. There are just **27)** .... birds walking around, looking for **28)** .... to eat. Time is passing but there still aren't **29)** .... trains coming!

E Put the verbs in brackets into the present simple or the present continuous.

A: What **30)** .... (you/eat)? It looks horrible.
B: My mum **31)** .... (say) it's good for me but I **32)** .... (not/think) it is.

A: Who **33)** .... (you/talk) to on the phone?
B: I **34)** .... (talk) to my mother. **35)** .... (you/want) to speak to her?

F **Put the verbs in brackets into the present simple or the present continuous.**

A: What **36)** .... (you/draw)?
B: It **37)** .... (be) a picture of my dad.
A: Where **38)** .... (you/work)?
B: I **39)** .... (have) a job in a supermarket but I **40)** .... (not/like) it, so I **41)** .... (look) for a new one at the moment.

G **Put the verbs in brackets into the present simple or the present continuous.**

42 They .... a film on TV at the moment. (watch)
43 Mum .... the washing-up now. (do)
44 He .... a game of tennis every Saturday afternoon. (play)
45 Every week she .... to the gym. (go)

H **Put the verbs in brackets into the present simple or the present continuous.**

46 Look at the cat! It .... onto the roof of the house. (climb)
47 Julia and Anna never .... coffee. (drink)
48 I always .... a black skirt and a green blouse at school. (wear)
49 Simon .... his little brother with his homework now. (help)

I **Fill in the blanks with the verbs from the list in the past simple. Use negations, too.**

cut be watch enjoy leave decide take have fall

Last night we **50)** .... anything special to do, so we **51)** .... to watch TV. The first programme **52)** .... terrible – we **53)** .... it at all. The next programme we **54)** .... was much better, though. It was about a girl who **55)** .... from a plane into the jungle. Some people found her and **56)** .... her to their village. They **57)** .... some branches and made her a hut. After several weeks some English people found her. When she **58)** ...., the villagers were very sorry to see her go.

J **Put the verbs in brackets into the present simple, the present continuous or the past simple.**

Last week we **59)** .... (go) to the beach. We **60)** .... (play) beach-volleyball and **61)** .... (swim) in the sea. Today we **62)** .... (go) to the country to visit my grandparents. The sun **63)** .... (shine). We usually **64)** .... (travel) by train, but today my father **65)** .... (drive) us there.

K Put the verbs in brackets into the present simple, the present continuous or the past simple.

Tony **66)** .... (play) tennis with his friend, George now. He **67)** .... (like) tennis and always **68)** .... (try) very hard to win. Last week he **69)** .... (lose) and he **70)** .... (be) very angry. But at the moment he **71)** .... (win) and he **72)** .... (be) happy. He **73)** .... (laugh) at his friend now.

L Choose the correct item.

74 Sally has two .... - a boy and a girl.
A child's **B** child **C** children

75 Is there .... Coke left in the bottle?
A any **B** none **C** little

76 I .... a good film yesterday.
A see **B** saw **C** am seeing

77 Harry is in bed; he ....
A sleeps **B** is sleeping **C** slept

78 There are .... people in the garden.
A some **B** any **C** nothing

79 He .... a book now.
A is reading **B** reads **C** read

80 She bought two .... of milk from the supermarket.
A pieces **B** slices **C** cartons

81 His name is Trevor. .... is very clever.
A His **B** Him **C** He

82 This is Lucy's dog. It's .... dog.
A she **B** her **C** hers

83 Would you like .... cup of tea?
A a **B** some **C** an

84 She went home two hours ....
A now **B** ago **C** then

85 I .... to Sally yesterday.
A speak **B** am speaking **C** spoke

86 Sue .... the Queen last year.
A is meeting **B** met **C** meets

87 Don't talk while you ....
A ate **B** are eating **C** eats

88 He .... three languages.
A is speaking **B** spoke **C** speaks

89 Do you know .... called Mike?
A anything **B** anyone **C** no one

90 Look outside! It ....
A is snowing **B** snowed **C** snows

91 Does she have a car? No, ...
A she doesn't **B** doesn't she
C she does

92 Sonia has .... of friends.
A some **B** lots **C** a few

93 Why ....? Do you know?
A she cries **B** she is crying
C is she crying

94 How .... sisters have you got?
A much **B** many **C** few

95 Harry .... his first day at school.
A remembers **B** remember
C is remembering

96 Yesterday, we .... to a restaurant.
A go **B** are going **C** went

97 I want to buy .... new books.
A no **B** some **C** any

98 Sue painted four little ....
A mouse **B** mice **C** mouse's

99 My mother's hair is very long. .... hair is beautiful.
A Her **B** His **C** Hers

100 Eva .... her bag last week.
A loses **B** is losing **C** lost

Pre-Test 3 (Units 1-12)

A Complete the text with the correct form of the verbs in brackets.

When I was young I **1)** .... (live) in Scotland. Now I live in France. I **2)** .... (be) in France for five years. I **3)** .... (move) here in 1997. My brother still lives in Scotland. He **4)** .... (visit) me many times. Last year he **5)** .... (stay) with me for a month.

B Complete the text with the correct form of the verbs in brackets.

Sally **6)** .... (work) as a doctor in Bristol since she **7)** .... (pass) her exams five years ago. She **8)** .... (study) Medicine at Bristol University. Actually she **9)** .... (live) in Bristol for ten years and likes it a lot. She **10)** .... (buy) a house there last year.

C Fill in since, for or ago.

11 I have know him .... five years.
12 She went to the cinema two days ....
13 They have been married .... twenty years.
14 We haven't seen her .... 1977.
15 I bought my car a month ....
16 I haven't eaten anything .... 10 o'clock.
17 I haven't been to work .... two days.
18 We haven't been on holiday .... 1988.

D Look at the pictures and write sentences using the *be going to* form, the present continuous or the present perfect.

19 (he/swim) ....
20 ....
21 ....

22 (she/eat) ....
23 ....
24 ....

E Fill in shall, will or the *be going to* form.

A: Your garden needs tidying.
B: I know. I **25)** .... do it this afternoon.
A: **26)** .... I lend you my gardening tools?
B: Thank you. I **27)** .... come round to collect them later.
A: I **28)** .... visit my brother this afternoon, so I **29)** .... bring them to you now, if you like.

F Complete the telephone conversation using shall, will or the *be going to* form.

A: **30)** .... I cook something for dinner?
B: No, thanks. I **31)** .... eat at a restaurant tonight.
A: Then I **32)** .... phone Chris and ask him to dinner.
B: He won't be at home. He **33)** .... meet me tonight. You can come, too.
A: Thanks. I **34)** .... see you at the restaurant, then.

G Write questions using the words in brackets.

35 Jim is going to eat a pizza. (What) ....?
36 I saw an old friend last week. (Who) ....?
37 Tom has got a radio. (computer) ....?
38 Jane cleans her room once a week. (How often) ....?
39 He works in a bank. (Where) ....?
40 I left school ten years ago. (When) ....?
41 Jill goes to the cinema once a month. (How often) ....?
42 I have been a teacher for ten years. (How long) ....?
43 Mike is going to cut the grass. (What) ....?
44 I saw my grandfather yesterday. (Who) ....?

H Look at the picture and fill in on, in, under or beside.

Tom is **45)** .... bed in hospital. The nurse is sitting **46)** .... his bed. There's a vase **47)** .... the table with some flowers **48)** .... it. Tom's slippers are **49)** .... his bed.

I Look at the picture and fill in on, in, under, beside or in front of.

This is Riverside Park. Some swans are swimming **50)** .... the bridge **51)** .... the river. There are some people standing **52)** .... the bridge. They are throwing bread to them. There's a van **53)** .... a tree. A man is selling ice-cream. A child is waiting **54)** .... the ice-cream van.

J Fill in on, in or at.

55) .... 1989, my husband and I went to Australia. We went 56) .... Christmas time. 57) .... Christmas Day we had dinner by the sea. We were still on the beach 58) .... 7 o'clock 59) .... the evening.

K Fill in on, in or at.

The library is open 60) .... Mondays, Wednesdays and Fridays. It opens 61) .... 9 o'clock 62) .... the morning. 63) .... Saturdays it is open until 2 o'clock. 64) .... July it closes for two weeks.

L Complete the text with the correct form of the verbs in brackets.

Sally 65) .... (live) in a flat on the third floor. At the moment she 66) .... (decorate) it for the party tonight. She hopes that a lot of people 67) .... (come). She 68) .... (already/buy) lots of food. Last year, forty people 69) .... (come) to her birthday party and they all 70) .... (have) a great time. Let's hope the party 71) .... (be) a big success as it 72) .... (be) last year.

M Complete the text with the correct form of the verbs in brackets.

I 73) .... (work) in an office in town. I 74) .... (start) my job two months ago. I think I 75) .... (stay) here for another ten months. I 76) .... (do) office work for two years, but at the moment I 77) .... (learn) how to use a computer. Every day I 78) .... (travel) to work by train. At the moment I 79) .... (save) money to buy a car. So far I 80) .... (save) £300.

N Choose the correct item.

81 I am going to America .... Christmas.
A at B on C in

82 .... did you phone her? This morning.
A Who B When C Why

83 The room is empty. There is .... there.
A no one B anyone C someone

84 I have been ill .... two weeks.
A for B since C yet

85 I .... to the shops yesterday.
A am going B went C go

86 John .... his homework yet.
A have not finished B is finishing
C hasn't finished

87 They are Julie's shoes. They're ....
A hers B her C she

88 I woke up ten minutes ....
A for B ago C since

89 There is .... bread left.
A few B a little C a few

90 I want to buy .... sweets.
A an B some C a

91 She .... her hat on the bus yesterday.
A left B leaves C has left

92 I last saw my dog two days ....
A ago B for C since

93 .... do you visit Ann? Every Friday.
A Why B How often C Who

94 That was my bike. It was ....
A my B mine C me

95 Do you need .... help with your homework?
A some B no C any

96 I heard a noise. There is .... in the cupboard.
A anything B something C nothing

97 My birthday is .... August.
A in B on C at

98 I don't think he .... the race.
A doesn't win B shall win C will win

99 I haven't made my bed ....
A since B for C yet

100 .... this film before?
A Do you see B Did you see
C Have you seen

Pre-Test 4 (Units 1-16)

A Match the sentences with the pictures, then identify the speech situation (request, suggestion or order).

Tidy your bedroom! **Would you take the dog for a walk, please?** **Let's walk to school.**

1 ....

....

2 ....

....

3 ....

....

B Match the sentences with the pictures, then identify the speech situation (request, suggestion or order).

Let's listen to some records. **Don't eat in here!** **Could you type the letters, please?**

4 ....

....

5 ....

....

6 ....

....

C Use comparisons to complete the text.

One of my friends has bought a new bike. She says that it is **7)** .... (good) her old one because it is **8)** .... (fast) the one she had before and not **9)** .... (small) as the old one. In fact her new bike is **10)** .... (fast) and **11)** .... (expensive) one in the village. I liked her other bike because it was a **12)** .... (nice) colour than her new one and it was **13)** .... (cheap) than that one. It also looked **14)** .... (beautiful) the new one, even though it was **15)** .... (slow) bike in the village.

D Use the comparative or superlative form of the adjectives in brackets to complete the text.

I come from a big family. I am 15 years old and I am **16)** .... (old) child in the family. I have two sisters and one brother, who are **17)** .... (young) me. Tania is **18)** .... (young) of all. She's only ten. John is fourteen but he is **19)** .... (tall) as I am. My other sister is Mary. She is twelve. We all go to the same school. John is **20)** .... (good) student in his class, but Mary isn't **21)** .... (good) as John. Her teacher says that she is **22)** .... (bad) in the class. Tania is a good student and she is **23)** .... (clever) in the class. We all love our school and I think it is **24)** .... (good) one in our town.

E Put the verbs in brackets into the infinitive form or the -ing form.

Philip loves **25)** .... (play) football. He wants **26)** .... (be) a footballer when he grows up. He hates **27)** .... (study) at school and he doesn't like **28)** .... (do) his homework. All he wants **29)** .... (do) is play football. He enjoys **30)** .... (watch) Manchester United and would love **31)** .... (watch) them play this Sunday, but he dislikes **32)** .... (travel) to the stadium, so he may watch the game on TV instead.

F Put the verbs in brackets into the infinitive form or the -ing form.

Sarah is very pretty. She wants **33)** .... (be) a model when she grows up. She loves **34)** .... (go) to fashion shows and **35)** .... (buy) all the fashion magazines. She always enjoys **36)** .... (watch) fashion programmes on TV. Sarah also likes **37)** .... (listen) to music and she hopes **38)** .... (start) music lessons this year. But her mother says that she must **39)** .... (work) harder at school, if she wants **40)** .... (have) these lessons.

G Complete the sentences with one of the modal verbs listed below:

must, mustn't, can, can't, could, needn't, will, won't

41 Dogs .... fly.
42 You .... wear a coat, it's quite warm.
43 Students .... be quiet when they take the test!
44 I .... go to school tomorrow because I am ill.
45 .... you open the window, please?
46 You .... drive fast. It's dangerous!
47 When he was fifteen he .... run fast but he can't now.
48 She's a famous ballerina. She .... dance very well.

(H) Complete the sentences with one of the modal verbs listed below:

must, mustn't, needn't, can, can't, couldn't, will, won't

49 She .... dance at the party because her leg was broken.
50 If you go to bed so late every day, of course you .... feel tired.
51 Your father is sleeping. You .... be noisy.
52 Birds .... fly.
53 If you don't study, you .... do very well in the test.
54 He is late; he .... run to school.
55 We .... book a table in the restaurant. John has already booked one for us.
56 Lions .... sing.

(I) Complete the sentences using too or enough.

57 "Can he buy the car?"
"No, he can't. The car is
......................................"
(expensive)

58 "Can she reach the cake?"
"No, she can't. She is
......................................"
(short)

59 "Can she wear the skirt?"
"Yes, she can. She is
......................................"
(thin)

(J) Complete the sentences using too or enough.

60 "Can he wear the shirt?"
"No, he can't. He is
......................................"
(fat)

61 "Can the cat catch the mouse?"
"No, it can't. The cat isn't
......................................"
(fast)

62 "Can she jump across the river?"
"No, she can't. The river is
......................................"
(wide)

(K) Choose the correct item.

63 Harry's birthday is .... February 18th.
A at B on C in

64 I like .... my brother's motorbike.
A riding B ride C rides

65 She is eating .... orange.
A a B an C –

66 We haven't got .... eggs to make an omelette.
A any B some C none

67 This is my sister's dog. It is ....
A her B hers C she

68 There's .... in the garden!
A somebody B anybody C no

69 Tom usually .... golf on Saturdays.
A has played B is playing C plays

70 I .... that film yet.
A didn't see B don't see
C haven't seen

71 They .... to the zoo yesterday.
A have gone B go C went

72 I will meet you .... 10 o'clock.
A at B on C in

73 She is the .... girl in our school.
A more beautiful B most beautiful
C as beautiful as

74 She met him .... Tuesday.
A at B on C in

75 You .... be late for school.
A must B needn't C mustn't

76 It usually snows .... winter.
A at B on C in

77 Peter is .... boy in the team.
A biggest B the biggest C bigger

78 Mr Morgan is my teacher. Do you know ....?
A his B him C he

79 I don't know .... at this party.
A anybody B somebody C nobody

80 A rabbit is .... than a lion.
A smallest B smaller
C the smallest

81 Frank is .... student in our class.
A the worse B worse than
C the worst

82 .... he like cats?
A Does B Do C Don't

83 They .... an expensive car last year.
A buy B bought
C have bought

84 I .... to Paris twice since 1980.
A went B go C have been

85 Could you lend me .... money, please?
A many B some C much

86 Mum .... her exercises at the moment.
A is doing B does C did

L Complete the passage with the correct form of the verbs in brackets.

Tony **87)** .... (work) in a bank two years ago. Now he **88)** .... (not/work) there because he **89)** .... (win) a lot of money one year ago. He **90)** .... (travel) to many countries since then but he **91)** .... (not/be) to America yet. He **92)** .... (already/decide) to fly to America where he thinks he **93)** .... (stay) for three weeks.

M Complete the passage with the correct form of the verbs in brackets.

Jim **94)** .... (work) in a shop since 1989. He **95)** .... (not/like) his job because he **96)** .... (not/earn) enough money. Yesterday he **97)** .... (have) an interview for another job in a bank. The interview **98)** .... (go) well and he **99)** .... (wait) for their answer at the moment. He hopes he **100)** .... (get) the job.

Progress Test 1 (Units 1-2)

NAME: .... DATE: ....

CLASS: .... MARK: ....

(Time: 30 minutes)

A Fill in a, an, or some.

1 .... girl 2 .... orange 3 .... octopus 4 .... cheese

B Fill in the plural.

5 one child - two ....
6 one cherry - two ....
7 one tooth - two ....
8 one mouse - two ....
9 one boy - two ....
10 one wolf - two ....
11 one brush - two ....
12 one man - two ....

C Fill in he, she, we, you or they.

13 balloons ....
14 Mary ....
15 brother ....
16 you and Bob ....
17 Tony and Bill ....
18 Steve and I ....

D Fill in, as in the example.

e.g.

A: Look at ...*it*...!
...*Is it*... a camera?
B: No, ...*it isn't*... .

19

A: Look at ....!
.... a nurse?
B: Yes, ...

20

A: Look at ....!
.... farmers?
B: Yes, ...

21

A: Look at ....!
.... dogs?
B: No, ...

22

A: Look at ....!
.... a cook?
B: Yes, ...

E Answer the questions, as in the example.

e.g.

A: Has he got a tray?
B: ...*Yes, he has*... .

23

A: Have they got tails?
B: ....

24

A: Have they got books?
B: ....

25

A: Has he got a camera?
B: ....

26

A: Has she got a cat?
B: ....

F Answer, as in the example.

e.g.

A: Can he paint?
B: ...*Yes, he can*... .

27

A: Can she type?
B: ....

28

A: Can he ski?
B: ....

29

A: Can they swim?
B: ....

30

A: Can she walk?
B: ....

Progress Test 2 (Units 3-4)

NAME:	**DATE:** ....
CLASS:	**MARK:** ....
	(Time: 30 minutes)

A Fill in my, your, his, her, our or their.

1 She's got an umbrella.
It's .... umbrella.

2 They've got a TV.
It's .... TV.

3 You've got a horse.
It's .... horse.

4 He's got a pencil.
It's .... pencil.

5 I've got a book.
It's .... book.

6 We've got hats.
They're .... hats.

B Underline the correct word.

7 My **sister's/sisters'** name is Sarah.

8 Her **friend's/friends'** names are Dan and Pete.

9 The **children's/childrens'** house is near the park.

10 Look at the **tree's trunk/trunk of the tree**.

11 His **mother's/mothers'** name is Joan.

12 His **brother's/brothers'** names are Kevin and Simon.

C Fill in a, an or the where necessary.

13 I saw .... elephant at the zoo.
14 This is .... my house.
15 .... Statue of Liberty is in .... America.
16 My neighbour is .... firefighter.
17 Tom has got .... bicycle.
18 .... blue jacket is mine.

D Fill in this, these, that or those.

19 .... are pears.

22 .... is a fish.

20 .... is a drum.

23 .... are balloons.

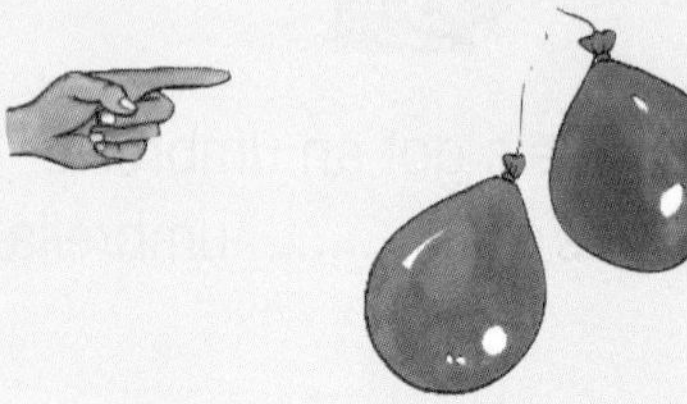

21 .... are squirrels.

24 .... is a key.

E Fill in a, an or some.

Linda: What is in that bag, Mum?
Mother: **25)** .... pen, **26)** .... sweets and **27)** .... envelope.
Linda: Is there anything else?
Mother: Yes. There is also **28)** .... book, **29)** .... stamps and **30)** .... orange handkerchief.
Linda: There are lots of things in your bag!

Progress Test 3 (Units 5-6)

NAME: .... DATE: ....

CLASS: .... MARK: ....

(Time: 30 minutes)

A Fill in much, many or a lot of.

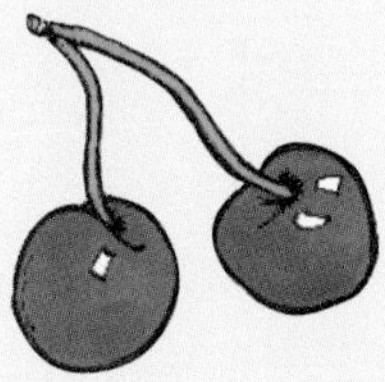

1 There aren't .... cherries.

2 There are .... grapes.

3 There isn't .... chocolate.

4 There's .... water.

5 There aren't .... bats.

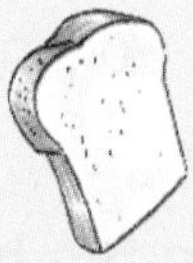

6 There isn't .... bread.

B Choose the correct item.

7 Have you got .... money?
A few B many C much

8 Can I have .... milk, please?
A many B a little C a few

9 How .... people are in the room?
A many B much C a little

10 There are .... biscuits in the tin.
A much B a few C a little

11 There are .... books on the shelf.
A little B much C a lot of

12 There is very .... honey in the jar.
A little B few C many

C Fill in some, any or no.

James: I'm hungry. Is there **13)** .... bread in the cupboard?
Paula: No, there isn't **14)** .... bread, but there is **15)** .... cheese in the fridge.
James: I don't want cheese. Are there **16)** .... biscuits?
Paula: No. There are **17)** .... biscuits, but there are **18)** .... apples.
James: OK. I'll have an apple.

D Write short answers, as in the example.

e.g. Do you like oranges? Yes, ...*I do*.... .

19 Does John play football on Saturdays? No, ...

20 Do you eat lunch at noon? Yes, ...

21 Are you a teacher? Yes, ...

22 Are they singers? No, ...

23 Do they visit their friends on Fridays? Yes, ...

24 Do you work on Sundays? No, ...

E Fill in the blanks with a verb from the list below in the present simple.

watch, be, practise, relax, go, get up

Jim McDonald **25)** .... a professional tennis player. Every day he **26)** .... at six o'clock. He **27)** .... with his coach all day and in the evening he **28)** .... He often **29)** .... TV. He always **30)** .... to bed early because he always feels tired.

Progress Test 4 (Units 7-8)

NAME:	**DATE:** ....
CLASS:	**MARK:** ....
	(Time: 30 minutes)

A Put the verbs in brackets into the present continuous.

1 Tom .... **(carry)** a tray.

2 Jane .... **(work)** on the computer.

3 He .... **(ski)**.

4 He .... **(paint)** a picture.

5 They .... **(swim)**.

6 They .... **(carry)** books.

B Put the verbs in brackets into the present continuous.

This is the dentist's surgery. A few people **7)** .... **(wait)** to see the dentist. Some children **8)** .... **(play)** and their mothers **9)** .... **(talk)** to each other. The receptionist **10)** .... **(answer)** the telephone. A young man **11)** .... **(read)** a magazine. The nurse **12)** .... **(come)** into the room to get the next patient.

C Choose the correct item.

13 Look at her! She .... a tree.
A climbing B climbs C is climbing

14 They .... for a test now.
A are studying B studying
C is studying

15 Johnny .... the dog at the moment.
A walking B walks C is walking

16 I .... my favourite book at the moment.
A read B am reading C reading

17 Look at them! They .... football.
A playing B are playing C play

18 The man in the bank .... money now.
A is counting B counts C counting

D Fill in the blanks with a verb from the list below in the past simple.

laugh, drink, go, drive, eat, see

Last Saturday I **19)** .... to the circus with my family. We **20)** .... the animals performing tricks and we **21)** .... at the clowns and their funny acts. We **22)** .... popcorn and we **23)** .... Coke. When the show was over, we **24)** .... home. It was a wonderful day!

E Put the verbs in brackets into the present continuous or the past simple.

Sandra **25)** .... **(wear)** a bandage on her arm because last week she **26)** .... **(fall)** off her bicycle and **27)** .... **(hurt)** it. At the moment she **28)** .... **(sit)** at home watching TV. Yesterday, her friends **29)** .... **(visit)** her at home. They **30)** .... **(take)** her some flowers and chocolates to cheer her up.

Progress Test 5 (Units 9-10)

NAME:	**DATE:** ....
CLASS:	**MARK:** ....
	(Time: 30 minutes)

A Answer the questions, as in the example.

e.g. Has Tom ever visited Paris? Yes, *he has.*

1 Has Lisa tidied her room? No, ...
2 Have the boys finished their homework? Yes, ...
3 Have you had a bath? Yes, ...
4 Has Robert broken the window? No, ...
5 Has Tim bought a new car? Yes, ...
6 Have Julie and Alan moved house? No, ...

B Fill in since or for.

7 They have lived in London .... 1987.
8 Paul and Lilian have known each other .... ten years.
9 Lucy has worked here .... two years.
10 She has had her car .... 1992.
11 Dan has been ill .... last week.
12 He has been a doctor .... six years.

C Fill in will or be going to in the correct form.

13 A: I've cut my finger!
B: I .... get a bandage.
14 A: These bags are very heavy.
B: I .... carry them for you.

15 A: What do you want to do when you leave university?
B: I .... be a teacher.

16 A: I promise I .... call you this evening.
B: OK. I'll be at home at seven o'clock.

17 A: I'll get the cake out of the oven.
B: Watch out! You .... burn yourself.

18 A: What are you doing on Saturday afternoon?
B: I .... visit my grandparents.

D Choose the correct item.

19 If you don't hurry, you .... late for school.
A are **B** have been **C** will be

20 Ruth .... me since October.
A hasn't phoned **B** won't phone **C** didn't phone

21 We .... a new film at the cinema tonight.
A have seen **B** are going to see **C** see

22 Watch out! You .... the plates.
A are going to drop **B** will drop **C** drop

23 Do you think it .... this winter?
A snowed **B** will snow **C** snows

24 David .... in that house for twenty years.
A is living **B** lives **C** has lived

25 .... you help me with the shopping tomorrow?
A Have **B** Shall **C** Will

E Fill in for, ever, already, yet or since.

26 I haven't finished my project ....
27 Have you .... been to Italy.
28 We have known each other .... we were children.
29 They have worked for that company .... two years.
30 She has .... done the washing and ironing.

Progress Test 6 (Units 11-12)

NAME: .... DATE: ....

CLASS: .... MARK: ....

(Time: 30 minutes)

A Fill in the correct preposition.

1 There is a vase .... the table.
2 There are some flowers .... the vase.
3 A cat is sitting .... the vase.
4 There is a bottle of milk .... the table.
5 A grey cat is .... the table.
6 The cupboards are .... the table.

B Fill in when, how, how many, how old, who, where, which or what time.

7 .... sisters has he got? Two.
8 .... do you live? In London.
9 .... does the film start? At seven o'clock.
10 .... is your birthday? 26th May.
11 .... is that man? My father.
12 .... are you? Fifteen.
13 .... do you feel today? Fine.
14 .... dress do you prefer? The red one.

C Fill in on, at or in.

15) .... Saturdays Freda is very busy. She gets up **16)** .... 8 o'clock and has breakfast. **17)** .... the morning she goes shopping and **18)** .... the afternoon she cleans the house. **19)** .... 7 o'clock in the evening she sits down to watch TV after a very tiring day.

D Choose the correct item.

20 '............... is this bag?' 'Paula's'
A Which B Whose C Who

21 .... are you laughing? Because that joke was funny.
A Why B How C Who

22 .... did you move to this town? Two months ago.
A How B Where C When

23 .... is your house? The one with the blue door.
A Which B What C Where

24 .... is that jacket? £25
A How B How many C How much

25 .... is your name? Amanda.
A What B Which C How

E Make questions for the following sentences, as in the example.

e.g. ...*Do you like pizza?* Yes, I like pizza.

26 ....? Yes, I live near the park.
27 ....? No, his favourite colour isn't blue.
28 ....? No, her name isn't Jane.
29 ....? Yes, they work in a bank.
30 ....? Yes, we like chocolate cake.

Progress Test 7 (Units 13-14)

NAME: .... **DATE:** ....

CLASS: .... **MARK:** ....

(Time: 30 minutes)

A Match the sentences with the pictures.

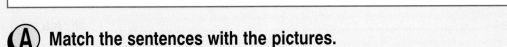

Pass me the salad, please!
Quick run away!
Would you type this, please?
Look out!
Don't take photographs!
Let's watch TV.

1 ....

2 ....

3 ....

4 ....

5 ....

6 ....

B Underline the correct item.

7 The children laughed **happy/happily**.
8 He always drives **careful/carefully**.
9 The test was very **easy/easily**.
10 Caroline is **beautiful/beautifully**.
11 Kevin shouted **angry/angrily**.
12 She always behaves **good/well**.

C Complete the sentences, as in the example.

e.g. Lisa earns *more* money *than* Emily. **(much)**

13 This is .... dress .... all. **(expensive)**
14 He is .... me. **(clever)**
15 She speaks .... him. **(quietly)**
16 Charles drives .... all. **(slowly)**
17 I run .... my sister. **(quickly)**
18 Their house is .... ours. **(modern)**

D Complete the sentences with in, of, than, as...as, or the.

My two best friends are called Daisy and Kate. We go to the same school. I'm older **19)** .... both of them. I'm **20)** .... tall .... Kate, but Daisy is **21)** .... tallest girl **22)** .... our class. Daisy and I are both clever, but I think Kate is the cleverest **23)** .... all. They are **24)** .... best friends I have ever had.

E Complete the letter.

Dear Chris,

I'm having a lovely time here in Spain. Last week it was warm, but this week it's **25)** .... **(hot)**. Everything here is **26)** .... **(beautiful)** than I imagined and Spanish food is **27)** .... **(tasty)** I have ever eaten. The beaches are lovely, but they're much **28)** .... **(busy)** than beaches in England. At the moment I am sitting next to the hotel swimming pool. It's **29)** .... **(big)** I've ever seen. This is probably **30)** .... **(good)** holiday I've ever had.

See you next week,
James

Progress Test 8 (Units 15-16)

NAME:	**DATE:** ....
CLASS:	**MARK:** ....
	(Time: 30 minutes)

A Put the verbs in brackets into the to-infinitive, the infinitive without to, or the -ing form.

Fred: Shall we **1)** .... **(go)** out tonight?
Rose: Yes. I would like **2)** .... **(have)** dinner at a restaurant.
Fred: I hate **3)** .... **(eat)** at restaurants, though.
Rose: Well, we could **4)** .... **(see)** a film instead.
Fred: That's a good idea. There's a new comedy on that I would like **5)** .... **(watch)**.
Rose: OK. Shall we **6)** .... **(buy)** a pizza on the way home?
Fred: Yes, that's a great idea.

B Complete the sentences with too or enough.

7 It's .... warm today to wear a coat.
8 I'm not old .... to go on holiday alone.
9 Sam didn't run fast .... to win the race.
10 My blouse is .... tight. I can't wear it any more.
11 They left early .... to catch the bus.
12 They've got .... money to go on holiday.

C Choose the correct item.

13 You .... go to the shops. I've already been.
A can't **B** mustn't **C** needn't

14 When I was young, I .... run very fast.
A can't **B** can **C** could

15 .... you like another biscuit?
A Shall **B** Will **C** Would

16 You .... take photographs inside the museum.
A shall **B** mustn't **C** would

17 She's very short. She .... reach the top shelf.
A can't **B** could **C** must

18 .... we go to the theatre on Saturday?
A Shall **B** Will **C** Would

19 Linda is an artist. She .... paint very well.
A couldn't **B** can **C** could

20 .... you help me with my homework, please?
A Needn't **B** Shall **C** Will

21 I tried to open the door, but I .... do it.
A can **B** couldn't **C** could

22 It's cold outside. You .... wear your gloves.
A must **B** can **C** mustn't

23 Policemen .... wear a uniform at work.
A mustn't **B** needn't **C** have to

D Fill in the correct modal verb.

24 .... you cook dinner tonight, please?
25 .... we have pizza for dinner? No, let's have steak.
26 You .... buy any bread. We've got plenty.
27 .... I borrow your pen, please?
28 She's ill. She .... stay in bed today.
29 You .... touch the oven. It's very hot.
30 I .... visit my grandmother tomorrow. My mother said so.

Word List

A

ability
abroad
actually
address
ago
album
allergic
alone
already
always
ambulance
ancient
anger
angry
ankle
arrive
art gallery
artist
as well
ash
assistant
at present
at the moment
avoid
awful

B

bald
bank
bank clerk
(be) sick of
behave
belong to
bench
besides
birdwatch
bite
blackberries
blouse
boat ride
bookshelf
bottom
branch
bridge
briefcase
bright
brush
bull
bunch
bushy tail

C

calculator
call
campaign
cap
career
careful
carelessly
carols
carpet
carry
cartoons
catch
catch a cold
chain
the Changing of the Guard
cheap
cheerful
Chemistry
chief
circle
classmate
clear
cliff
climb
collect
(come) past
comfortable
comparative
compare
comparison
compartment
consonant
contact lenses
cook
cooker
copy
cottage
couch
crisps
cry
customer
cycle

D

dangerous
decide
deer
degree
dentist
develop
directly
disappear
discuss
distance
divide
don't worry
drop
during

E

earn
either
else
engine
enjoy
envelope
ever
every
everyone
evidence
except
excited
exciting
exotic
expensive
experience
explore
express

F

fabulous
faint
fall down
famous
far
farm
farmer
feed
field
fill in
finally
fire brigade
fire-station
fishing rod
fit
flashing
flat
flight
flour
for
forget
fork
form
freeze
fry
funny
funny cartoon
furniture

G

gardener
gate
gentle
get divorced
get engaged to
get into
get off
get out
ghost
gift
gloves
gold
gossip
grow
grow up
guard
guest
gun
gym

H

habitual
hairbrush
half-way
handkerchief
hard
hard working
hay
headache
health
height
helpful
hide-and-seek
hit
hit song
hole
honeymoon
hope
horrible
housewife
how long
humour
hurry
husband

I

ice-rink
ice-skating
immediately
implication
in pen
in pencil
include
information
information board
inspector
instead
instruction
instrument
intelligent
interesting
invite
iron

J

journey
jumper
jungle
just

K

keep fit
kennel
kind

L

land
last
later
laugh
laugh at
lawyer
lecture
lie
light
lion tamer
loaf
loan
lock up
lollipop
long
look after
look forward to
louse
lovely
luckily

M

magazine
magazine rack
mammal
map
marry
material
medal
mend
merry
message

midnight
milk
millionairess
mirage
miserable
miss
mix
mother tongue
motorcycle
moustache
move
musical

N

nap
narrow
nearby
necessity
neighbour
neighbourhood
never
next
noise
northern
notebook
now
nut

O

object
obligation
often
oil
on foot
on my own
order
or else
otherwise
outdoor
oversleep
ox

P

pack up
paint
passenger
Passport Control
peace
peach
penguin
pepper
permanent
permission
pet
petrol
pick up
pie
plant
plenty of
polite
politely
popular
possess
prediction
prefer
present
private
probably
proof
puncture
puppy
put on
put the fire out
put up a tent

Q

qualifications
quantity
quarrel
quickly
quiet

R

race
racing car
rack
raisin
rarely
rather
reach
realise
recently
regret
Relax!
report
request
resolution
result
return
rifle
rob
rock
roof
rose
row
rude
rudely
rug
run away
runner

S

sailing
salary
Sales Department
salt
scare away
scientist
scream
seat
secret agent
security guard
seem
seldom
sell
sense
serious
serve
sewing machine
shed
shine
shoot
shopkeeper
shopping list
shout
show
sign
silver
simple
since
sleeping bag
slide
smart
sneeze
snow
so far
sofa
sometimes
soon
sort out
spacesuit
spelling
spot
stable
state
steak
stethoscope
story-teller
strange
strawberry
subject
success
suitcase
sunbathe
sunny
suntan
suntan cream
superlative
suspect
sweater
sweets
swimming pool
swing
switch
syllable

T

take off
team
temperature
temporary
tent
terrible
terrorist
then
threat
ticket
ticket-inspector
tidy
tomorrow
tonight
toothache
tour
towards
toyshop
tractor
traditional
traffic
travel
tray
tube
turn
turn off
turn on
type
typewriter
typist

U

underline
uniform
union
unique
university
upstairs
use
usually

V

villager
visitor
vowel

W

waiter
warm
warning
watch
watch out
wave
wear
wedding anniversary
weight
welcome
wet
when
while
(it's) windy
wonderful
wood
World Championship
wrong

Y

yesterday
yet